DESIGNED to SELL

> smart ideas that pay off!

Meredith® Books
Des Moines, Iowa

Editor: Vicki Christian
Contributing Writer: Jody Garlock
Contributing Designers: Dan Fish, John Jensen, Chad Johnston, On-Purpos, Inc.
Copy Chief: Terri Fredrickson
Publishing Operations Manager: Karen Schirm
Senior Editor, Asset and Information Manager: Phillip Morgan
Edit and Design Production Coordinator: Mary Lee Gavin
Editorial Assistant: Kaye Chabot
Book Production Managers: Pam Kvitne, Marjorie J. Schenkelberg, Rick von Holdt, Mark Weaver
Contributing Copy Editor: Susan Fagan
Contributing Proofreaders: Beth Havey, Amy LaMar, Kenya McCullum
Contributing Photographer: Michael Garland
Photo Stylists: Kimber Blake, Elizabeth Sloan-Freel
Indexer: Jana Finnegan

Meredith₀ Books
Executive Director, Editorial: Gregory H. Kayko
Executive Director, Design: Matt Strelecki
Managing Editor: Amy Tincher-Durik
Executive Editor, Group Manager: Denise Caringer
Senior Associate Design Director: Doug Samuelson
Marketing Product Manager: Tyler Woods

Publisher and Editor in Chief: James D. Blume
Editorial Director: Linda Raglan Cunningham
Executive Director, New Business Development: Todd M. Davis
Executive Director, Sales: Ken Zagor
Director, Operations: George A. Susral
Director, Production: Douglas M. Johnston
Director, Marketing: Amy Nichols
Business Director: Jim Leonard

Vice President and General Manager: Douglas J. Guendel

Meredith Publishing Group
President: Jack Griffin
Executive Vice President: Bob Mate

Meredith Corporation
Chairman and Chief Executive Officer: William T. Kerr
President and Chief Operating Officer: Stephen M. Lacy

In Memoriam: E.T. Meredith III (1933–2003)

Library of Congress Control Number: 2005929390
ISBN 13: 978-0-696-22450-8
ISBN 10: 0-696-22450-X

All of us at Meredith₀ Books are dedicated to providing you with information and ideas to enhance your home. We welcome your comments and suggestions. Write to us at: Meredith Books, Home Decorating and Design Editorial Department, 1716 Locust St., Des Moines, IA 50309-3023.

All materials provided in this book by or on behalf of HGTV or otherwise associated with HGTV's program *Designed to Sell* and owned by Scripps Networks, Inc. are used under license by Meredith Corporation. "HGTV," "Home & Garden Television," the HGTV logo, and the title "Designed to Sell" are service marks and/or trademarks of Scripps Networks, Inc.

Designed to Sell is produced by Pie Town Productions.

I confess: Before I became host of the HGTV series *Designed to Sell*, I couldn't have been convinced to do anything to my house before selling it. After all, who has the time, money, or energy these days? But thanks to the design magic of Lisa LaPorta (aka Elastic Lisa who can stretch a budget) and the brutally honest room critiques of real estate experts Donna and Shannon Freeman, I have been a witness to wealth time and again. Who would ever have thought that such a small investment—just $2,000—in sprucing up a home could bring such a juicy return?

Consider me a convert. I'll never again unwittingly plunk a "For Sale" sign in my yard without first having perked up my property similar to how it's done on *Designed to Sell*. The quick tips (who knew you should turn on every light in the house before showing it to make it seem bigger and brighter?) and sage advice (you mean, you have to *stage* your rooms?) are invaluable lessons.

Though watching homeowners go from utterly (or clutterly) challenged to organized and richer in 30 minutes of television is very entertaining, we knew many of you clamored for more. So we created this book. We've packaged some of the best *Designed to Sell* makeovers, tips, and tricks in these pages so everything will be at your fingertips.

Speaking of making money, there's another type of richness associated with *Designed to Sell* that gives me enormous pleasure. When I arrive to tape the open house segment of the show, the sellers are seeing the dramatic transformation for the first time. They often say to me, "Why didn't we live like this in the first place?" They fall in love with their home one last time. By heeding the lessons on the show and in this book, we can make our daily lives a little better—a little richer.

Whether you are "designing to sell" or "designing to keep," this book carries through the show's trademark enthusiasm and savvy, budget-friendly approach to decorating. Not only should you do everything we recommend, you *must* do it to win the real estate game. Remember, we have the proof that sweat-equity and cosmetic improvements pay off. See you at the open house!

CLIVE PEARSE Host, *Designed to Sell*

>CONTENTS

> READY, SET, SELL!

On every episode of the hit HGTV show *Designed to Sell*, homeowners preparing to sell their houses fling open their doors to professionals who are ready to scrutinize and revitalize. After a frank assessment from real estate experts Donna Freeman or Shannon Freeman and a stylish spruce-up plan from interior designer Lisa LaPorta, the *Designed to Sell* team gets down to business—painting and primping to ready rooms for the open house. The time frame? Two days. The budget? $2,000. The results? Amazing! With their homes looking better than ever, sellers have walked away with thousands—even tens of thousands—of unexpected dollars.

> "When home buyers see a maintained home, they figure this house is worth the asking price."
>
> —designer Lisa LaPorta

> "Buyers are swayed by the decor of a home."
>
> —real estate expert Donna Freeman

The lessons learned on the show work for any homeowner—whether the plan is to sell next month, next year, next decade, or further down the road. (After all today's smart decisions are tomorrow's cha-ching when a buyer signs on the dotted line.) The beauty of the *Designed to Sell* approach is that it's attainable, and dramatic results are possible with even a modest $2,000 budget. "Two thousand dollars can make a dent in the worst-case scenario, and it can make a dent in the best-case scenario," Lisa says.

The proof is in the sale. The revamped rooms enable the sellers to raise their asking price. The home's inviting new look often causes a bidding war in which the sellers end up with more money than they asked for—and more than they ever imagined possible.

Intriguing? Yes. But *Designed to Sell* is more than entertaining television. Each episode is packed with ideas to help anyone who is stuck in a decorating rut.

Is your dated kitchen the last place you'd go to enjoy a meal? Do you cringe when you pull into the driveway, witnessing a front door with tarnished hardware? Is your guest bedroom a dumping ground for discards from other rooms?

All the decorating inspiration you need is inside this book. So, too, is a wealth of advice from Lisa, Donna, Shannon, and host Clive Pearse, who share their favorite tips for making a home not only look better, but function better too.

˅ inside this book

Consider this book your road map for getting top dollar—or maximum enjoyment, as the case may be—from your home. For some, the destination is just around the corner as you're preparing to list your house. Others may be delaying the selling journey until retirement.

For ease in helping you tackle trouble spots, this book is divided into chapters categorized by room. If your bathroom is your home's weakest link, for example, turn to the "Kitchens and Baths" chapter beginning on page 98. Here, as in each chapter, you'll find inspiring before-and-after photos, with "The Makeover" helping you navigate how it was done. In "What's Wrong With This Room?" you'll learn Donna or Shannon's assessment, which could just as well be coming from your own agent or a candid friend. The "Lessons Learned" at the end of each room tour offers general tips for getting your house ready to sell as well as time-tested design advice.

The makeovers aren't the end-all of this book. In the "Do It Yourself" chapter beginning on page 176, you'll find projects that are sure to come in handy, such as stripping wallpaper and installing a self-adhesive vinyl tile floor—both of which the *Designed to Sell* team is well-versed in doing. And of course, insight from the *Designed to Sell* experts is woven throughout these pages to inspire you to get your rooms looking their best.

X Start!

MONDAY | TUESDAY | WEDNESDAY | THURSDAY | FRIDAY

declutter | more declutter | CLEAN! | CLEAN!

SATURDAY | Notes: | SUNDAY

CLEAN!

fix faucet

> get moving

Whatever stage you're at—packing boxes or just longing to make your house a more enjoyable place to call home until that fateful day arrives—take some cues from *Designed to Sell*. These strategies will get you thinking about what to do and help jump-start your journey.

PRETEND THERE'S A HIDDEN CAMERA What would people say about your home if they thought you weren't there? Would they make fun of the kitschy wallpaper or the grandmotherly draperies? Would they take note of the dirty windows and dog hair coating the sofa? Take a tour of your home from a buyer's perspective. Or, like on *Designed to Sell,* have a real estate agent point out things that are sure to turn off buyers. If you're not at the agent stage, a candid friend or relative can offer advice—just promise not to hold their comments against them.

RANK YOUR ROOMS Trying to tackle all of your home's shortcomings at once is overwhelming. On *Designed to Sell,* the focus is on two, sometimes three, areas most in need of an overhaul. Rank your rooms, putting the most-neglected ones or ones that would give the biggest payback at the top of the list, then work your way down the list. You may only have time to finish the top one or two.

CHECK THE CALENDAR Set a budget and a time frame for getting the work done. Be realistic. If you're listing your house in two months, a new hardwood floor makes no sense financially or timewise. But if you plan to stay put for a few years, that wood floor could be a smart move. You'll get to enjoy the beauty, and hardwood floors have great appeal to buyers.

> look at **the big picture**

On *Designed to Sell,* it's common to hear Lisa and Clive tell the weary—and sometimes leery—homeowners (after all, seeing their house torn apart can be daunting) to stay focused on the big picture. That's perhaps the best advice of all. As you start the revamping process, let the end result motivate you. Imagine finally getting the cluttered desk moved out of the dining room so you can enjoy quiet meals there, or having the neighbors comment on how great your landscaping looks and how inviting the front porch is.

Few people have the luxury of a team of Lisas, Clives, Donnas, and Shannons who can spot shortcomings and make improvements. Still, you can crack the whip on your own. Consider these ideas:

IF YOU HAVE A MONTH...
> Clear clutter.
> Clean everything, including windows and carpeting. Budget permitting, hire a cleaning service.
> Focus on the kitchen and the main bathroom—two rooms that help sell a house.
> Fix obvious flaws, such as a leaky faucet or a hole in a wall.
> Remove wallpaper from and/or paint at least one room.
> Revamp outdated sink fixtures.
> Add curb appeal by painting the front door and updating the hardware on it.

IF YOU HAVE A YEAR...
> Remove all wallpaper; paint all walls and ceilings.
> Replace worn or dated flooring in at least one room.
> Commit to a large improvement you've been delaying, such as painting your home's exterior.
> Complete unfinished projects, such as installing a chair rail in the dining room or landscaping the side yard.
> Declutter and clean.

IF YOU HAVE MORE THAN A YEAR...
> Establish a plan for tackling areas that need the most attention, based on your priorities list.
> Remodel a room. Low- to mid-range kitchen and bath remodels have the biggest payback. New siding is another improvement with payback.
> Keep up with maintenance to avoid costly and time-consuming repairs when you're getting ready to sell.
> Schedule annual or biennial safety and maintenance home inspections and have the furnace serviced annually to help extend its life.
> Whittle clutter annually by holding a garage sale or donating items. (There's nothing more daunting than clearing through a lifetime of accumulations when it's time to sell.)

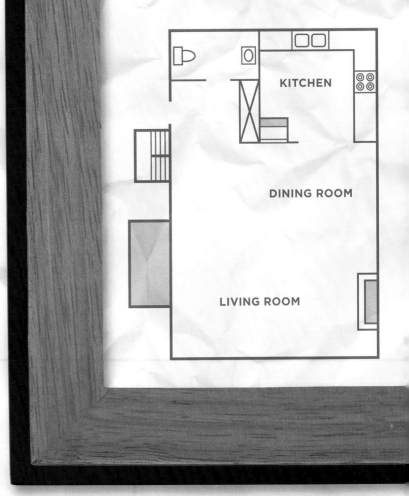

> Establish a cleaning routine. For example set aside Thursday evenings for cleaning the kitchen, Saturday mornings for the garage, and so forth.

READ ON! The "Getting Started" chapter, beginning on page 12, will help prepare you for the nitty-gritty of the selling process, such as choosing an agent, setting a price, and staging your rooms. Then let the room makeovers, beginning on page 30, motivate your redecorating. Heed the lessons, and you'll see your home in a whole new light—perhaps one with bigger dollar signs attached or one that's now so enjoyable to live in you'll decide to take down the "For Sale" sign.

> MEET THE TEAM

SHANNON FREEMAN

Shannon Freeman jokes that she became a real estate agent when she was 3 years old. That stems from a childhood traipsing along with her mother and fellow *Designed to Sell* agent Donna Freeman. Though real estate was in her blood, Shannon didn't decide to make a go of it until after she graduated from college. With eight years "officially" under her belt, Shannon knows how to make a home appeal to the masses to generate a "buzz" about it. Fans of the show know better than to be fooled by Shannon's California-girl-next-door looks. She has mastered the art of giving a painful analysis with a loving smile—including in her mother's home. Her latest coup was coaxing Donna to update the dated almond-color switchplates and outlets in her home with bright white ones. When not verbally critiquing each other's homes or those on *Designed to Sell,* the sharp-tongued duo pen a newspaper column called "House Rules." Visit Shannon at www.donna-shannon.com

DONNA FREEMAN

Veteran real estate agent Donna Freeman sums up a home seller's biggest mistake in two words: litter box. Such succinct and brutally truthful observations have earned Donna a loyal following of fans eager to hear what will roll off her tongue next. With nearly 30 years of experience to tap into, Donna knows the importance of show—and signs of furry four-legged friends aren't what buyers want to see. The Oklahoma transplant has trained her daughter and *Designed to Sell* cohort, Shannon Freeman, to also tell it like she sees it. Though Donna (www.donna-shannon.com) knows that home ownership is still the great American Dream, she's dumbfounded that real estate has become such a hot topic. "People are obsessed with real estate," she says. "Even when we go out socially, people ask us about it. We sometimes make up fake occupations just to get away from talking about it."

CLIVE PEARSE

British-born Clive Pearse now calls sunny California home. His charming accent and quick wit have made the *Designed to Sell* host wildly popular with the home buyers he meets at open houses, as well as fans of the show. Clive is best known in Europe for his award-winning cult TV show *On The Air,* a radio-style call-in show, and two prime-time TV series for NBC Europe. During his *Entertainment X-Press* stint, he covered Hollywood happenings and interviewed stars like Meryl Streep and Tom Hanks. On *Ushuaia,* he interviewed world-class adventurers and boldly (and usually unsuccessfully) attempted challenging stunts himself, including a narrow escape from a hot-air balloon crash. Clive also has developed a successful voice-over career, lending his talents to television and radio commercials for such clients as Jaguar, Land Rover, Ziploc, and to movies, including characterizations for the Oscar-winning *Shrek.* Clive, who lives in Los Angeles, recently became an American citizen. Visit Clive at www.clivepearse.com.

LISA LAPORTA

Making $2,000 look like a million bucks isn't easy, but interior designer Lisa LaPorta does it week in and week out on *Designed to Sell.* Her amazing makeovers are responsible for awed homeowners getting multiple offers and raking in more money than they ever imagined possible, as well as for inspiring TV viewers to spruce up their own homes. Many of Lisa's tips—such as removing heavy window treatments that block light—don't even cost a penny. Lisa, who calls Los Angeles home, received her formal training in design from UCLA's Department of Environmental Art and Design, and has appeared on several HGTV shows, including *Designers' Challenge* and *Designing for the Sexes.* Lisa has a lifelong passion for all types of design, art, architecture, and music. She is a Latin scholar who knows the best museums, shoe stores, and sidewalk pizza places in Florence, Italy.

GETTING STARTED

From choosing an agent to staging your rooms, here's the know-how you need to sweep buyers off their feet.

>DECISIONS
DECISIONS

You've decided to sell your house … now what? Should you hire a real estate agent? Should you start sprucing things up—like painting walls or laying new tiles? Or should you begin the arduous task of sorting and packing? The answer is yes, yes, and yes!

The *Designed to Sell* team knows how emotional selling a house can be. Team members have consoled teary-eyed homeowners and, conversely, they've had to practically strap paintbrushes to the hands of a few disengaged sellers. "Many home sellers are already looking toward the new home and they've sort of emotionally checked out of the place they're living in," interior designer Lisa LaPorta says. "It's a costly mistake."

To ensure you're up to the task—and clear headed enough to make smart and swift decisions—answer these questions:

> **AM I EMOTIONALLY READY?** Whether you're selling for a straightforward reason like a job relocation or you're on the fence about listing, get your emotions in check so you can get top dollar. "It's like going into business with yourself," host Clive Pearse says. "You have to draw the line on the 'We live here' to 'Now we're in business.'" After sprucing up your home, you may realize that everything you were looking for was there all along—it just needed better packaging. Whether you're selling or staying, you'll have created a win-win situation.

> **AM I WILLING TO INVEST TIME AND MONEY?** Getting a house ready to sell is a full-time job, with a burgeoning "expense account" for paint and other supplies. Keep in mind that you have to spend money to make money. If you don't have the time yourself, figure out what the labor costs will be.

> **CAN I LIVE IN A FISHBOWL?** Sellers struggle with their lifestyles being inconvenienced while their house is on the market. Remember you're "designing to sell" not "designing to live." How you approach the process is your call. "It really comes down to how much [sellers] are willing to forgo in bottom-line profits versus not having their daily life altered," says real estate expert Donna Freeman. "Some people are willing to 'pay' that extra money with a lower sales price so that their life is not disturbed."

"When you sell your house, there are many layers and aspects to what is going on," real estate expert Shannon Freeman says. "A wrong choice of an agent could be a financial disaster."

> choosing an agent

As much as people like to complain about the commissions real estate agents charge (commonly 5 percent or more of the selling price, split between the seller's and the buyer's agents), about 90 percent of sellers use agents. There's good reason: An agent shoulders stresses that would otherwise fall on you. When you're trying to spruce up your house and then keep it spotless, having to field calls from strangers and wade through paperwork filled with legalese only makes the blood pressure rise. "When you sell your house, there are many layers and aspects to what is going on," real estate expert Shannon Freeman says. "A wrong choice of an agent could be a financial disaster."

How can you find a good agent? Consider these options:

> **ASK AROUND.** Get the names of agents from friends, relatives, neighbors, and coworkers. Find out what they did and didn't like about their agent. A good indicator is whether they would use the person again.

> **ATTEND OPEN HOUSES.** Even if you're not considering purchasing a specific house, you may find an agent you like. The way they interact with you is how they'll interact with potential buyers for your own house. A pushy agent may be a turnoff, while a laid-back one who does little to tout the house's features may be too lax.

"It's like going into business with yourself," host Clive Pearse says about selling a home. "You have to draw the line on the 'We live here' to 'Now we're in business.'"

> clive's quick tips

To get the selling process off to a good start, consider these tips from *Designed to Sell* host Clive Pearse:

> **GET A BLUNT, FRESH OPINION ABOUT YOUR HOUSE.** If you take it the right way, constructive criticism can help put money in your pocket.

> **ADJUST YOUR ATTITUDE.** Your home is now a commodity.

> **LET IT GO.** Be willing to get rid of things that are cluttering your home and complicating your life.

> **KNOCK YOURSELF OUT.** When you feel too tired to drag on, remind yourself that sweat-equity is a good investment.

DESIGNED TO SELLISM

BOLD COLORS = FEWER BUYERS. Neutral colors have widespread appeal. If you simply can't find the time to repaint a bold-color room, tone down the intensity by bringing in darker furnishings, fabrics, and accessories.

> **OBSERVE FOR SALE SIGNS.** Agents' names usually are included on the sale signs in sellers' yards. Pay attention to the names and which signs are—and aren't— quickly covered with "sold" signs.

The Freemans recommend interviewing at least three agents, paying close attention to the person's communication style, demeanor, and character. "They are acting on your behalf, so you better like all of these things," Donna says. Make sure the agent is licensed and, ideally, does the job full-time. The person should show knowledge of such things as loans, appraisals, disclosure laws, and title issues.

"Agents wear many hats, and they must have all the resources to get the job done, and also act as an emotional sounding board for the sellers because they are typically going through a big change in their life by selling what is usually their biggest asset," Shannon says.

Like houses, agents come in different forms—as do the agencies (brokers) they work for. Traditional agents earn a commission, and tend to offer full services. Flat-fee agents charge a predetermined amount for selling your home, regardless of the selling price; services are more limited. You may be responsible for holding your own open house, and you may pay an extra fee to get your home listed on the Multiple Listing Service, a broad listing of homes that most agents use.

A seller's agent represents sellers; that person's loyalties are to you. A buyer's agent represents the buyer. Sometimes, the seller and buyer end up with the same agent. This is where things get dicey. If your agent also represents the person who wants to make an offer on your house, how do you know the agent hasn't mentioned what your bottom line is? Obviously a higher selling price is to the agent's advantage, but a quick sale can be enticing too. Most states require agents to disclose the type of agent they are. In the case of an agent ending up representing both parties, the agent must disclose at the time the offer is presented who he or she represents—the buyer or seller. If it's not you, think through the offer thoroughly, because at this point your agent is working to get the best deal for his or her other client.

> setting the price

You know what you paid for your house, and you probably have a pretty good idea of how much you have put into it over the years. But it's not as simple as combining those two figures and maybe adding a little cushion to determine your asking price. Times change. Mortgage rates rise and fall. Property appreciates and depreciates in value. That value is really nothing more than someone's opinion of your home's worth. And that someone is the buyer.

Though there's no single formula for figuring out what price tag to put on your home, there are variables that should—and shouldn't—weigh into your pricing decision.

> **FORGET THE PAST.** The current marketplace—the here and now—overrides how much you paid for your home and how much you've spent improving it. Have your agent prepare a comparative market analysis to show the selling prices of similar homes in your neighborhood. More telling is what they sold for in comparison with the asking price. This so-called "price spread" indicates if your neighborhood is hot, warm, or cold.

> **REMOVE THE EMOTIONS.** The fact that you did the landscaping yourself or that this is your childhood home means nothing to buyers. Sentimental attachments can interfere with logic.

> **KNOW YOUR COMPETITION.** Visit open houses to get an idea of how your home compares with others in looks, condition, and price. If there are a glut of homes for sale in your neighborhood, you need something to set yours apart. It doesn't necessarily have to be a lower price; a stylish, immaculate home is priceless.

> **ASK YOUR AGENT.** Veteran agents have a sort of sixth sense about pricing. Ask your agent or the agents you're considering what they think your house is worth. In the process, the agent can point out things that may be dragging the price down—and that are fixable so you can increase the price.

> **DON'T BE ALOOF.** Buyers, not you, ultimately set the price of your home. That's why a well-maintained home that looks good is crucial.

> questions to ask prospective agents

Include these key questions when interviewing a real estate agent, and use the answers to gauge your comfort level with their skills.

> Are you licensed?

> How long have you been an agent? Is this your full-time job?

> How many homes have you listed in the past year? How many have you sold? What was the average price?

> What's the average length of time it takes you to sell a house?

> Do you have a specialty, such as townhouses, starter homes, or million-dollar homes?

> Will you provide a comparative market analysis? (This is a common comparison of recently sold houses in a neighborhood, and is something every agent can—and should—easily provide.)

> reality check

To be a good seller, think like a buyer. You may have your own idea of reality, but a buyer's perception is the only reality that counts. Ponder the following scenarios, and let the lessons help guide your fix-up decisions.

SELLER'S REALITY: Two dogs, two cats, three birds, and four gerbils make for one happy home.

BUYER'S PERCEPTION: Is this a zoo? Is that a urine stain I see on the carpeting? Has a cat been clawing up the curtains? My, this house stinks.

THE LESSON: A home filled with pets sends red flags, even to animal-loving buyers. Clean carpets and draperies to remove pet odors and stains. Move food bowls and litter boxes to out-of-way places. If possible, find a temporary home for caged animals and remove four-legged friends from the home when potential buyers visit.

SELLER'S REALITY: Forget the outside—I'm too busy painting inside to worry about it.

BUYER'S PERCEPTION: It's not the nicest-looking house around. Look at those weeds. And the front door and those shutters really need painting. I'm not sure it's worth coming back for the open house.

THE LESSON: Curb appeal counts. Even if you only have time to trim the lawn, paint the front door and shutters, and place a container of flowers by the door, do it. Buyers will be scoping out your property even before the open house. If the exterior isn't welcoming, they may never step foot inside.

SELLER'S REALITY: Yikes! The open house is tomorrow. I'll shove everything into the closets.

BUYER'S PERCEPTION: These closets are stuffed to the max. This house obviously doesn't have enough storage space.

THE LESSON: Buyers will be opening up closet and cupboard doors, so keep them tidy. Purge your home of excess, rather than shoving it behind closed doors. Take it to a storage facility for safekeeping.

SELLER'S REALITY: The house down the street just sold for $400,000, so I'll ask that for mine.

BUYER'S PERCEPTION: There was a house down the street that just sold for what these sellers are asking, but it had two more bedrooms, a spa master bath, and a gourmet kitchen. These sellers obviously are trying to scam us.

THE LESSON: Compare apples to apples. Have a comparative market analysis done on your home, and go to open houses of similar homes so you can make a visual analysis too.

DESIGNED TO SELLISM

WHEN IN DOUBT, TAKE IT OUT. Too much stuff in a room (even in closets and cupboards) gives buyers the impression of a too-small house with not enough storage space.

> room to improve

Even without the Freemans' frank advice, you probably are aware of your home's problem areas, such as the mauve carpeting or the harvest gold appliances Less obvious is what improvements will give you the most bang for your buck. There's good news: "Anything you do to your home is never a waste of money—unless it's an indulgent, personal statement," Lisa says. (Read that this way: Resist the urge to splurge on bright blue countertops. Instead, install neutral-color ones that have mass appeal.)

In most cases cosmetic improvements are a financially better and highly effective alternative to remodeling or spending big bucks on structural updates. "Buying a home is an emotional decision—either the buyer likes the feel of the house or not," Donna says. "The feeling that buyers get is from the cosmetic aesthetics of a house, not from a really snazzy roof. Buyers are swayed by the decor of a home."

To improve your home's appearance, consider Lisa's design advice:

> **START OUTSIDE.** Though Lisa usually is inside a home wielding paintbrushes and sliding sofas, home sellers can take a more outwardly approach. "Curb appeal is number one," she says. "Curb appeal can kill or make a sale." Even if new siding or paint is out of the question, there are small things you can do to improve your home's appearance. Start by creating a welcoming front entry by painting the door and adding a container or two of colorful flowers. (For more on curb appeal, see the exteriors section beginning on page 178 of the "Do-It-Yourself" chapter.)

> **HAVE A PAINT PARTY.** Nothing updates a room faster or cheaper than paint. It makes a house seem newer and smell fresher. Choose neutral colors (they have universal appeal), but steer clear of play-it-safe white, which is stark. "You're selling a package and an environment that people would want to spend time in," Lisa says. "White walls are not the most appealing." She opts for warm neutrals—golden beiges and sandy tans—that have a bit of a kick. (For Lisa's favorite paint colors, see the "Walls" section beginning on page 182 of the "Do-It-Yourself" chapter.)

> **GET COOKING.** Kitchens are hot commodities in today's homes. "If a kitchen is old, I recommend changing it," Lisa says. "You'll get money back and have a quicker sale because of it." New appliances top her to-do list. Even if they aren't included in the asking price, a new fridge and stove update the overall look of the room. Floors are key too. Lisa considers ceramic or stone tile a great investment, but she knows inexpensive self-adhesive vinyl tiles can do the job in a pinch. Paint works wonders on dated cabinets.

> **BRING ON THE BLING.** Sink faucets, light fixtures, doorknobs, and cabinet pulls are boring stuff, right? Not to Lisa, who refers to these items as "jewelry for the home." Adding new pulls to a lackluster bathroom vanity or a new handle to the front door may be the little bit of sparkle your home needs to attract potential buyers.

> the freemans' fab four

What are the top things you can do to make your house show better? *Designed to Sell's* resident agents Donna and Shannon Freeman consider these as musts:

1 Finish any incomplete home improvement projects.

2 Paint walls. A bonus is that fresh paint has a subliminal smell that sends a "Wow, this is new" signal to house hunters.

3 Replace dirty or worn floors; thoroughly clean existing ones.

4 Green up the lawn and plant flowers in the landscaping.

> GET ORGANIZED

So much to do, so little time. Once you've decided to sell your house, you may feel like you've stepped onto a roller coaster. Paperwork and calls from agents and buyers flood in, boxes must be packed, clutter has to be cleared—and then there's an entire house that requires your attention so you can get that windfall from the big sale.

Though it may sound contradictory, taking some time to get organized before you jump into your long list of home improvement projects or before you head to the nearest paint store will save you time in the long run. Boxing up knickknacks, for example, will make your home seem less cluttered (good for buyers) and you'll have one fewer box to pack when moving day approaches (good for you).

The following approaches from professional organizer Vicki Norris, president of Portland-based Restoring Order, will make the selling and moving processes work in tandem.

> **FACTOR IN FUNCTION.** Remind yourself of the purpose of each space in your home, and how the items in that space serve that purpose. Move items that support those activities into the appropriate room. If you primarily listen to music and watch movies in the family room, for example, gather up all the CDs and DVDs from other rooms and keep them there. From a selling standpoint, having a designated room for every item is key to minimizing clutter. From a moving standpoint, grouping similar items together makes it easy to take inventory and decide whether to pitch or pack things.

The items should be packed together with a destination room in mind.

> **MAKE LISTS.** As you determine what belongs in each space, develop a to-do list of repairs and improvements. Look beyond the obvious, such as dated wallpaper or cracks in walls. Do the rooms have proper lighting? Are tobacco or pet odors present? Does the space have an inviting aesthetic?

> **PRIORITIZE.** Like those on *Designed to Sell,* most homes have more projects than can feasibly be done in the allotted time or budget. Therefore

> be it hereby resolved...

Getting organized and staying organized are two different things. These strategies will help you with both.

> Create a binder or accordion file for the paperwork pertaining to the house you're selling and the one you're buying. Having agent agreements, disclosure statements, inspection reports, and so forth at your fingertips will come in handy whenever there's a question.

> Wash and put away dishes as soon as you've finished a meal. If you use a dishwasher, run it and empty it before you go to bed.

> Discard magazines and newspapers that are more than a week old. If you haven't read them yet, you probably won't get around to it.

> Pay bills as soon as they arrive in the mail to prevent piles from forming. If you're stashing bills in drawers every time you show your house, you're more likely to lose them and end up paying a late fee.

> When you buy something new, get rid of something old.

> Stay out of stores. Going to the mall or your favorite boutiques only invites the temptation to buy something and bring it into your home. An exception to this rule are hardware stores and home centers, which you'll likely frequent to purchase materials and paints to spruce up your house.

> Put things back where you got them. Enough said.

> Learn to say no. Resist taking freebies from store vendors or keeping ones that come in the mail or land on your doorstep, such as shampoo samples with the Sunday newspaper.

> And learn when to say yes. If a charity calls to say it will be in your neighborhood to pick up items for donation, schedule a time. Even if you're not sure what you have to donate, the appointment is incentive to purge. (And you have free delivery to unload the sofa that's merely holding clutter in your basement.)

> Allot 15 minutes at the end of each day to make a quick run-through of your home to tidy it up.

prioritize the items on your list. It's a good idea—even a profitable one—to consult with your agent or other professional to determine what buyers' hot buttons are so you can match their wants to your to-do list. Assign a completion date and budget for each project, based on its priority, then work accordingly—or schedule appointments to have fix things that require special skills.

> **PURGE, PURGE, PURGE.** Getting rid of the excess has big payoffs. You'll be able to show buyers a tidy, and hence a visually larger house. And you won't have to use your valuable time to move things to a house where they'll get neglected once again. To make it easier to part with

items, donate them to a charity—there's something freeing about giving things to people or organizations who can really use the items. While you're in clear-out mode, tackle the overload in a storage rental or a friend's basement. Most people seldom need—and may not even recall—what they've already put out of their minds.

Granted, putting the above into practice is easier said than done. Purging can be a painful process, as is accepting the differences between being a seller and being a dweller. Interior designer Lisa LaPorta has a quick reminder to anyone who is struggling to make the transition: "It's not *Designed to Live*; it's *Designed to Sell*," she says. "You can keep your TV and baskets of laundry, but it will cost you."

> "It's not *Designed to Live;* it's *Designed to Sell*," interior designer Lisa LaPorta says. "You can keep your TV and baskets of laundry, but it will cost you."

> conquering clutter

You may feel good about keeping up with the Joneses, but the end result is a house stuffed to the rafters. And that gives buyers the impression of too little house with too little storage space. Stop the insanity! "Clutter is a virus that seems to be going around," says real estate expert Shannon Freeman.

The problem extends beyond the knickknacks and items stuffed in closets and drawers. Clutter also takes the form of too many—or too large—furnishings crammed into a room or items you use daily—the coffee maker on the countertop, the shampoo bottles in the shower, the paper shredder in the guest bedroom

that also pulls duty as the home office. A home that's clutter-free gives buyers the impression—real or imagined—of a well-tended house. After all a homeowner who makes the effort to keep closets and cupboards orderly certainly makes sure the roof isn't leaking and the furnace is clean, right?

Consider these savvy approaches to corralling clutter.

> **START SMALL.** Arm yourself with garbage bags—the musts on every professional organizer's list—and go on a room-by-room pitching mission. If you're struggling to part with things, ask yourself, "What's the

worst thing that could possibly happen if I get rid of this?" Start at one end of the room or concentrate on a certain element, such as a drawer or closet. The goal is to handle each item as few times as possible. If something is in the wrong spot—say a screwdriver in a bedside nightstand—put it in a bag or box labeled "relocate." Don't waste time taking each stray item to its proper home; wait until the bag or box is filled to do that.

> **EDIT FURNISHINGS.** Think "less is more" with furniture. Often, half of the furnishings you have in a room can go, and the room will be better because of it.

DESIGNED TO SELLISM

WHERE'S THE STORAGE? If you think you're being smart by shoving stuff under beds or in other awkward spaces, think again. Buyers may interpret this as a sign that the home lacks storage space.

Remember, you're selling a house, not a furniture store. Decide which items are key to making the room look its best—not which ones make your life more enjoyable. (See more furniture tips in the "It's Show Time" section beginning on page 24.)

> **BE STORAGE SAVVY.** There's a hierarchy to storage. Obviously the things you use daily should get prime billing in cabinets and drawers. You may need to spend some time reorganizing for function and practicality while you're showing your home. For example relocating the toaster from the countertop to a cupboard may require getting rid of seldom-used things stored there.

> **RETHINK YOUR LIVING.** An always-tidy home is the bane of every seller's existence, but get used to it. Put hobbies on hold—you won't have time for them anyway—so you don't have piles of books stacked by the sofa or a partially completed puzzle on the dining room table. Before you turn the lights out for the night, tidy up.

> the ultimate clutter buster

Holding a garage sale or tag sale while you're preparing to put your house on the market isn't ideal timing, but sometimes it's necessary. The money you make can help offset the costs of your home improvements. Consider these tag sale tips.

> **PRICE TO SELL.** This is no time to try to get top dollar (or dime) out of a five-year-old bridesmaid's dress or a trolling motor you never use.

> **OFFER A FREE BOX.** Bargain hunters can't pass up a box marked "free," so put one out front to lure people to your sale. Restock the box throughout the day; you may have to move some of the items you're trying to sell into it. "Free" boxes are a great way to unload things you may not have thought about, such as partially used gallons of paint and leftover wallpaper. You'll gain buyer-pleasing space in your basement or garage!

> **MAKE A POST-SALE PLAN.** Pledge that the things you don't sell won't come back inside your house. Load the items into your car immediately after the sale as incentive to get them to the nearest charitable drop-off point as soon as possible.

> IT'S SHOW TIME!

After the paint buckets are drip-dry and the lawn is a lush emerald green carpet, you may be tempted to open the door in the excitement of having crossed off everything on your to-do list. Not so fast! No seller worth his or her lockbox would let agents and prospective buyers inside without first partaking in a friendly little game of illusion known as staging. Once your rooms are properly staged, then bring on the open house!

Staging is essentially making your home look like a model home—making it look just lived-in enough, but not shabby and disorganized, says real estate expert Donna Freeman. "It's like creating a fantasy for a buyer—a lifestyle and home life that they would like to purchase," she says. And which is more likely to get top dollar from buyers: a home with dirty dishes, smelly litter boxes, and clothes heaped by the washing machine, or one with sparkling clean surfaces, bouquets of fresh flowers, and the smell of fresh-baked cookies wafting through the air?

Stripped of the reality of daily life, a staged home tends to sell faster and for a higher price. That's why many agents consider staging as a mandatory final step before showing your house.

DESIGNED TO SELLISM

ONE PURPOSE PER ROOM, PLEASE. Buyers shouldn't have to work to figure out how a home can function for them, so make sure each room has a clear identity.

> setting the stage

The goal with staging is twofold: First you want to accentuate your home's best features and downplay its negatives. Furniture placement, paint color, and accessories all help accomplish this. Second you want to depersonalize your home to give it widespread appeal and to give buyers a sense of belonging. Personal items—such as photos filling shelves or invitations stuck on the refrigerator— are distracting; curious buyers may spend more time trying to piece together your life story than noting the great built-ins or the high-end refrigerator you're throwing in as part of the deal.

Specific staging examples are woven throughout the room makeovers in the following chapters. Combine them with these general staging guidelines to make your place seem like home sweet home:

> **STRIVE FOR MODEL BEHAVIOR.** With their lived-in-but-no-one-lives-there feel, model homes enable buyers to imagine themselves there. They're great examples of proper staging: Furniture is placed to allow easy traffic flow, there's no guesswork about each room's purpose, and everything is accessorized to emphasize the home's extras, be it a fireplace or a jetted tub. There's a bit of trickery too: The scale of furnishings is usually on the small side so rooms feel larger. Contrast a model home to

> lisa's freebies

Is style for free too good to be true? Not to interior designer Lisa LaPorta. Let her zero-dollar improvements for staging or transforming a room inspire other decorating ideas on the cheap:

1 Get rid of 25 to 50 percent of the stuff in each room. People just have too many things in their rooms, Lisa says.

2 Rearrange furniture. Furniture that hugs the walls (Lisa's pet peeve) creates wasted space in the center of the room. Move it around to savor square footage.

3 Clean windows inside and out. The room will feel brighter and bigger because of it, she says.

4 Borrow from friends. Ratty, old furniture is a big buyer turnoff. "People see old furnishings and read the same thing into the house," Lisa says. Ask friends for loaners so you can compile a temporary new ensemble.

your own. Does oversize furniture make the walls feel like they're closing in? Does the plethora of photos on the mantel make your eye gravitate toward the pictures instead of the mantel itself? Let model homes be a cue for staging your own rooms.

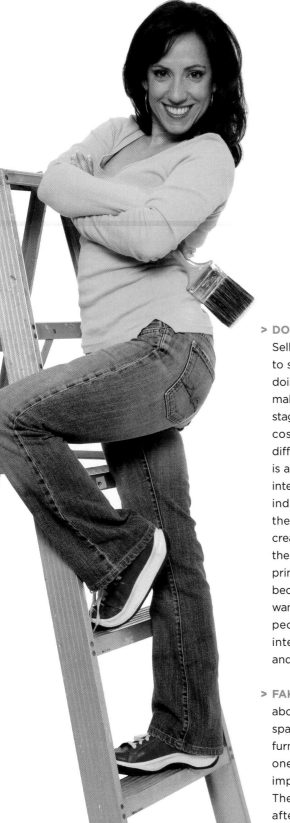

"The single-handed biggest mistake home sellers make is to think that they need to do nothing," says interior designer Lisa LaPorta. "They'll think 'It's been good enough for me all this time, why isn't it good enough for somebody else?'"

> **DON'T BLUR THE BOUNDARIES.** Sellers who consider staging a chance to showcase their personal style—as in doing some interior design work—are making a big mistake. Even though staging and interior design both involve cosmetic changes, there are key differences between the two. Staging is about appealing to the masses, while interior design is about appealing to individual tastes. Those who realize the difference—and opt for staging to create widespread appeal—will reap the rewards. "When you stage, you are priming something that is going to become a market commodity, and you want that priming to appeal to as many people as possible so that you will interest as many people as possible and get lots of offers," Donna says.

> **FAKE THE MOVING DAY.** Staging is about illusions, and the illusion of more space should be a priority. Removing furnishings that are too large or simply one too many for a room gives the impression of added square footage. The elimination process—especially after you've already whittled and

cleared clutter—can be brutal. A 6-foot armoire that stows your electronics may be your most-used item, but if it's taking up a good chunk of a room and impeding traffic flow, it needs to find a new home. Even small changes— removing a nightstand, coffee table, or ottoman—can visually expand a room. Your home's square footage is prime real estate, and every item in it must earn its keep.

> **KEEP IT CLEAN.** It goes without saying that a house that's for sale needs to be spotless in every nook and cranny. Clean, though, is also a style of sorts. Think simplicity when you're staging. A window treatment comprised of swags, jabots, panels, and sheers can look fussy and block light. Remove the outer treatments and let the sheers go solo. *Voila!* The room is brighter and cleaner—and a buyer's mind is less cluttered and freer to make a big purchasing decision.

> **HAVE A PURPOSE.** When you're staging a room, think about function, purpose, and logic. Every room needs an identity so buyers don't have to guess what they'd use it for. If a dining room is your makeshift office, turn it back into its intended purpose. Dining rooms always have selling power and buyers won't have to wonder where they'll eat their meals or entertain guests. Be cautious of and do some careful staging in rooms that serve dual purposes. You don't want to inadvertently send a signal to buyers that the house isn't big enough for multiple functions or to accommodate a growing family.

> **PAINT A PICTURE.** Consider yourself an artist and your house your canvas. Then fill in the blanks to bring your picture to life. A patio is just a cold stone slab until you paint it with a pitcher of lemonade, a magazine holder next to an Adirondack chair, and pots of colorful flowers. Your goal as an artist is to create a warm and inviting setting that will make house hunters want to linger. Stage every room with that goal in mind, be it with pillows, cozy throws, candles, or logs stacked in a firebox.

> **CREATE A "SCENT-SATION."** What house hunters smell is as important as what they see. Make sure your home passes the sniff test. Forget frying up bacon—or any other strong-odor foods—on open house day. Bake a batch of cookies, a pie, or bread to stir up homey scents that appeal to their emotions. Don't go overboard; too much aroma may make buyers think you have something to hide—which begs the question: Do you? Odors from smokers, pets, or damp rooms can torpedo offers. You may be immune to the smells, so have a neutral third-party take a whiff, and then take corrective measures. New carpet, paint, and a dehumidifier may all be in order.

> tidy-up tips

Keeping your house buyer-ready is a 24/7 task. This checklist will help keep you on track so you'll be ready at a moment's notice if a potential buyer or agent calls.

DO THIS DAILY...

> Make the beds.

> Get clothes off floors and into a hamper or back on hangers.

> Hang towels and wash rags on towel bars to dry; put in hamper when dry.

> Give tubs, showers, sinks, and ovens a light scrubbing after use.

> Wash dishes or put them in the dishwasher as soon as a meal is done.

> Sort and file or dispose of mail as soon as you get it.

> Find a home for everything. Newspapers go in the recycling bin, coats and shoes go in the closet, dirty clothes go in the hamper—no exceptions!

> Put away personal items, such as eyeglasses and magazines on a nightstand and lotions and toothbrushes on a bathroom vanity.

DO THIS WEEKLY...

> Tend to the yard (mow lawn, water plants, pick up debris).

> Dust, vacuum, and sweep bare floors (do more often if needed).

> Lightly scrub refrigerator and oven.

> Shake throw rugs; vacuum or wash if very dirty.

KEEP A CLOSE WATCH ON...

> **Windows and light fixtures.** Clean as needed. Even lightbulbs need dusting.

> **Laundry.** Don't let it pile up in a heap on floors or by the washing machine.

> **The dishwasher.** Empty it as soon as dishes are clean; letting clean dishes sit there encourages dirty ones to pile up in the sink.

> **Food bowls and litter boxes for pets.** Put them in an out-of-the-way place, and keep the area around them clean. Remove them entirely during an open house or whenever the house is being shown to potential buyers.

> **Odors.** Avoid cooking foods that leave strong odors, such as bacon or fish. If you must cook them, open windows, if possible, or light a fragrant candle to mask smells.

> **The thermostat.** Try to maintain a comfortable temperature level so the house isn't overly hot or cold—neither of which are inviting.

> **The garage and basement.** It's easy for these spaces to become the new home for items you've cleared from other rooms. If the garage or basement is overly crowded and you simply cannot part with things permanently, rent a storage unit so you don't give buyers the impression that the house lacks space.

For Clive Pearse it's one of the ironies of selling a home: The owner can spend thousands of dollars replacing the roof or updating the electrical system, but it's the little cosmetic changes that will catch buyers' attention, appealing to their emotions and leading to an offer. As *Designed to Sell* host and open house guru, Clive has witnessed cosmetic karma time and again. Buyers who see a deer head hanging on a wall may flee a home that's in great shape structurally, and instead make an offer on a beautifully decorated home with a leaky roof and cracking foundation. The biggest mistake home sellers make? "They underestimate the little things," Clive says. "If you slap on a new knob or handle on a cabinet, buyers will say 'Oh, this place is so nice.'"

> the open house

At long last, you're open for business—the business of selling your house! When the open house rolls around, real estate experts Donna and Shannon Freeman recommend that you turn on all the lights (brighter is always better). In addition play classical music softly in the background, place some vases of fresh flowers or bowls of fresh fruit in strategic places, bake some cookies, and then make yourself (and your pets) scarce. Hovering homeowners can be the demise of a deal.

That said you still should take precautions by storing valuable items in a safe deposit box or a relative's home. "Open houses can oftentimes get busy and the agent can't keep an eye on everyone at all times," Shannon says.

Though open houses are considered a conventional part of the selling process, few homes are actually sold at them. "Open houses are for nosy neighbors and lookey-loos for the most part," Shannon says. Nevertheless they have their merits, as many of the *Designed to Sell* homeowners can attest. A sometimes overlooked virtue is that the open house forces you to get your act together; it's your drop-dead completion date.

Agent tours called "brokers' opens" are one form of an open house that can be a gold mine for reaching serious buyers. Have your agent arrange a day for other agents to view your house—typically before an open house is scheduled. Those agents then spread the word to their clients. (Also make sure your agent lists your house on a Multiple Listing Service, a widely used computer-based program that allows agents to share and track listings.)

Both the conventional open house and the brokers' opens help to create a "buzz" about your house—hype to draw house hunters inside. After all the best staging in the world won't make a bit of difference if there's no one to see the great results.

To help drum up interest, you or your agent will need to have data sheets—known as "sell sheets"—on hand to distribute at the open house or to make available by the "For Sale" sign in your yard. As such, know what's expected and the ramifications of your words.

> **BE ON THE UP AND UP.** If your house is 1,700 square feet, should you just round up to 2,000? Can the room in the basement be considered an additional bedroom, even if it doesn't have an egress window? The answer to both is no. It's never a good idea to fudge when giving your home's vital stats. The same goes for its physical condition—the state of the roof, any problems with termites, and so forth. Get familiar with the disclosure laws in your state, and get your agent's advice on how to present things. "When in doubt, disclose it," Donna advises. "Just put it out there for the buyers. If it scares the buyer away, then they were not the right one for you." Pleading ignorance isn't a defense—even if you're just a

DESIGNED TO SELLISM

SMALL PROBLEMS ADD UP TO BIG MESSES. As buyers tour a house, they make mental lists of the little fix-ups that need to be done. A multitude of minor repairs add up to one whopping project. Take care of those nagging flaws before you show your house so buyers aren't distracted or dissuaded by them.

wee-bit off on something. "Ignorance is not bliss, it's deadly," Donna says.

> **HIT THE HOT BUTTONS.** If you've got it, flaunt it. Hardwood floors, fireplaces, and walk-in closets are three features that buyers love. New sells too: If you've remodeled, replaced carpet, reroofed—you name it—point that out on your sell sheet or in your ad.

> **BE SPECIFIC.** Though you need to be concise when describing your home, don't be vague. A gourmet kitchen may sound great on paper, but it doesn't mean much to buyers. Provide the juicy details. Granite countertops, cherry cabinets, and stainless-steel appliances, for example, are features buyers can envision.

> **CHOOSE YOUR WORDS WISELY.** Certain words and phrases are red flags to buyers—you should know, you've scoured the classified ads before. A "charming bungalow" is usually interpreted as a small house; a "do-it-yourselfer's dream" is a fixer-upper nightmare. Always put a positive spin

"When in doubt, disclose it," Donna Freeman advises. *"Just put it out there for the buyers. If it scares the buyer away, then they were not the right ones for you."*

on things. An undecorated home is "ready for buyers to put their stamp on." Buyers tend to think with their hearts, so appeal to their emotions. A "tree-lined street" or a "wraparound porch with a great view" may motivate them to pick up the phone or hop in the car. Start and end with a bang; studies show that people remember the first and last things they read.

> **INCLUDE THE BASICS.** House hunters have a price range and an idea of the neighborhood they want to live in, so include your asking price and address on your sell sheets or in ads. If you don't, you'll waste time taking calls.

Ready to see how home sellers have cashed in? Turn the page to start your tour of some hot properties from *Designed to Sell.*

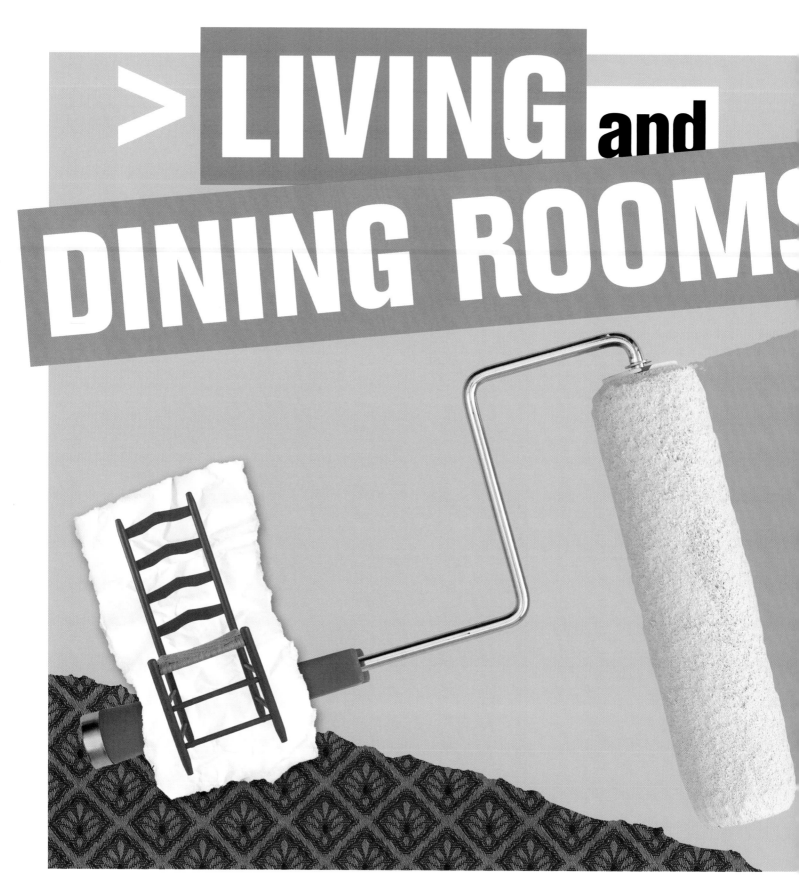

> LIVING and DINING ROOMS

Formal or casual, living and dining rooms need to roll with style. These makeovers set the standard in furniture placement, accessorizing, and more.

> perfect fit

Good things come to those who listen to what a room tells them. This space screamed for furnishings that wouldn't overpower it or detract from sought-after features, including a fireplace and wood floors.

BEFORE

WHAT'S WRONG with this room? Real estate expert Donna Freeman's positive first impression of this home quickly vanished when she stepped through the front door and immediately into the living room. "I didn't know we were coming to a funeral home," she says of the space that featured an oversize black sectional draped with throws and overall drab decor.

To showcase the fireplace, Lisa created a conversation area toward the center of the room, flanking the fireplace. Though personal photos can be distracting to house hunters, the large photo propped on the mantel is an effective way to draw attention to the fireplace without the added expense of new artwork.

ACTION PLAN Find the right fit. The room's oversize furnishings, including a sofa the homeowners dubbed the "black beast," overwhelmed the space and gave it a cluttered, somewhat claustrophobic feel.

RIGHT: Strategic use of pattern calls attention to key features. The area rug that anchors the sitting area draws the eye to the wood floor—a popular feature with home buyers. Conversely the plaid cornices draw the eye upward to showcase the height of the windows.

"We maximized the size of the room, changed the layout, and really drew attention to the fireplace."
—designer Lisa LaPorta

RIGHT: Upholstered cornices teamed with billowy drapery panels give the windows— and the room in general— a stylish update. Plaid is a timeless pattern with gender-neutral appeal.

THE MAKEOVER Knowing that downsizing the decor was key to giving this living room selling strength, interior designer Lisa LaPorta splurged on new furnishings. Her goal was twofold: Smaller furnishings would visually expand the space and showcase the room's strongest features—a fireplace and wood floor. The $673 price tag of the smaller-scale pieces was worth it, because they allow the eye to move more freely around the room and give the illusion of added square footage. Grouping furniture into a centrally located conversation area added coziness. Dated window treatments got the boot, and a fresh coat of paint on the walls created a warm backdrop. "We maximized the size of the room, changed the layout, and really drew attention to the fireplace," Lisa says.

> in proportion

In room design, proportion refers to how furnishings look in relation to each other and to the room itself. The most eye-pleasing arrangements appear compatible in scale. Though you should try to strike a pleasing balance when you're getting ready to show your house, there are special considerations to take as a seller.

> Remember that bigger furnishings aren't necessarily better because they make rooms appear smaller. Look for ways to "trim" big items. For example, remove a piece of a huge sectional to turn it into two smaller loveseats or place some pieces in storage.

> Consider the visual weight of furnishings. Even if two coffee tables are the same size, a glass-top one with slim metal legs will appear less bulky than a solid wood one.

> Go easy on accessories. Reserve disproportionately small collectibles for a glass display case or a shadowbox. Better yet, pack them up now; small knickknacks give rooms a cluttered look.

> Build a room around a key item. Designate a must-have piece of furniture, such as a bed or sofa, and then add or subtract other elements based on how they fit with the main piece.

> budget breakdown

Furniture	$673
Window treatments	$245
Paint and supplies	$40
Sconces	$60
Accessories	$5
Total	$1,023

CHA-CHING! The changes in the living room—along with those made in the master bedroom (see "Elegant Upgrade," page 138) and bath (see "Clean Sweep," page 118), gained an overall decluttering of the home—resulted in multiple offers. And the sellers get $50,000 above the price of other homes in the area.

OPPOSITE: Mirrors hung on the wall behind the sofa, and clear glass pieces placed on the coffee table bounce light around the room. **RIGHT:** Well-edited accessories contribute to the room's streamlined look while also providing color and texture for visual interest.

> lessons learned

> MAKE A GOOD FIRST IMPRESSION. Regardless of how great a home looks from the outside, the first step inside is telling. This crucial initial encounter should send a positive vibe and put house hunters in a good mood—or at least a more forgiving mood—as they scrutinize the rest of the home. Lisa sunk about half of her $2,000 budget for the entire house into the living room to transform it into a warm, welcoming space that instantly will strike a chord with potential buyers.

> DO THE FURNITURE SHUFFLE. Even if you're convinced there's only one way to arrange the furnishings in a room, try, try, and try again. The *Designed to Sell* team members

moved furnishings around until they found the perfectly choreographed placement. The process took them full-circle: In the end they reverted to the first arrangement they tried. Your goal as a seller is to position furnishings to capitalize on or at least not to block the room's best features, such as a window or fireplace. Be prepared to remove furniture from a room too; less is more when you're in selling mode. These homeowners temporarily parted with their large entertainment center that detracted from the fireplace.

> CREATE COZINESS. Two sofas, grounded by an area rug, face off in this room to create an intimate conversation area. Adding an area rug is an easy and

effective way to carve a special area out of a larger space. A coat of mellow golden-tone paint on the walls also adds warmth and coziness.

> BE A FASHION-FORWARD SELLER. It didn't take a trained eye to realize that droopy drapes were dragging this room down. The scarf-style valances were simply outdated in both style and color. Strive to do something about your room's dated elements. The solution may be simpler than you realize. If you have a great view or handsome windows, for example, no window treatment is usually better than one that screams 1980s. Outdated decor sends a signal that your home is yesterday's news.

> separate but equal

When there are no walls separating a living and dining room, it's easy for one space to dominate. This living room had crept over the visual boundary, leaving little space for dining. Given equal footing from a function and style standpoint, this dual-purpose room is user friendly and buyer-ready.

BEFORE

WHAT'S WRONG with this room? With the living room furniture crowding out the dining area—which had nothing more than a hard-to-access table—this room had confusion written all over it. "If I saw 'dining room' listed on a flyer and I walked in and saw this, I'd be really disappointed," real estate expert Shannon Freeman says. "Buyers are trying to imagine themselves in this house, and if they can't see themselves sitting there, they're going to think 'Where am I going to eat?'" Like the dining area, the living room's fireplace was visually lost. Instead the attention focused on a television positioned in front of a window unfortunately dressed with a fussy treatment. The window treatment, along with stained carpeting, robbed the room of natural light and likely would drag down the home's selling price in the process.

New bookcases that resemble built-ins draw the eye to the fireplace and bring function to a formerly empty recessed corner to the right of the fireplace. "They actually spread out the living room," Lisa says. "They make it feel so much richer, much more custom. The corner no longer feels like a corner, but part of the room." The crown molding that tops each bookcase complements the molding on the mantel for a seamless integration. The bookcases are constructed from plywood, a strong and budget-friendly material.

ACTION PLAN Carve out more style. Both the dining area and the fireplace require more of a presence. The decor, including the carpeting, needs to be updated to give the space a refreshed look.

"When people see custom items, such as bookcases, they assess value."

—designer Lisa LaPorta

THE MAKEOVER Heeding Shannon's advice to pull every penny of value out of the fireplace, interior designer Lisa LaPorta assigned some carpentry work to the *Designed to Sell* team. Floor-to-ceiling bookshelves now flank the fireplace to draw attention to this sought-after feature. "When people see custom items, such as bookcases, they assess value," Lisa says. Painted white and topped with crown molding to complement the mantel, the bookcases have the feel of expensive built-ins. "Precision is the key," Lisa says. "Built-ins only score big if they blend with the home's architecture." Furniture was positioned to draw the eye toward the fireplace, rather than a television. In the dining area, Lisa positioned a new dining set—smaller and sporting cleaner lines than the previous one—below a stylish iron chandelier that replaced a formal crystal one. The revamped arrangement takes the guesswork out of where the dining room is—or if there's really one at all.

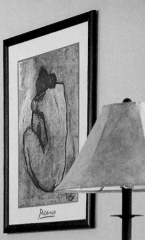

Neutral-color walls and carpeting make this room move-in ready. Venture beyond whites, and instead choose neutrals with warm undertones to help cast your rooms as comforting, cozy spaces.

> temperature control

In the rush to get paint on the walls, clear clutter, and make everything squeaky clean, home sellers sometimes overlook a minor thing that can add or detract from the ambiance: room temperature. Before buyers parade through your house, set the thermostat so rooms are neither too hot nor too cold. "It is so important when you're selling a house to have the environment completely comfortable," interior designer Lisa LaPorta says.

OPPOSITE TOP AND LEFT: The floor-to-ceiling bookcase and the angled chair define the boundary between the living and dining areas. A crackling fire adds ambiance and helps buyers envision relaxing evenings at home. Don't leave anything to chance when showing your house, though. Unless you or another adult will be standing guard, forgo lighting a fire. Staging the firebox with logs can help conjure a similar peaceful image.

> budget breakdown

Living room furniture	$820
Dining area table and chairs	$325
Lumber and supplies	$250
Dining area lighting	$128
Window treatments	$75
Paint and supplies	$60
Living room lighting	$33
Total	**$1,691**

CHA-CHING! Lisa's confidence in sinking nearly all of her $2,000 budget into this one room proved to be worth the risk. Two weeks after the open house, the townhouse sold for $30,000 more than similar ones in the complex. (To see how Lisa revamped the kitchen for less than $200, see "Living Larger," page 106.)

Once squeezed out by the living room, the dining area now has a clear identity. The new dining set is centered below a stylish chandelier that creates a focal point and establishes the space's domain. Before the makeover, chairs backed against the wall offered little function.

FAR LEFT AND LEFT: A classic-looking window treatment frames sliding glass doors—a decorating troublespot for many homeowners who default to style-deprived vertical blinds. The valance hangs high above the doors so as not to interfere with the door's movement. Lisa steered clear of frilly, feminine fabrics, yet brought florals into the mix with the earthy valance fabric. The fabric reappears as banding along the sides and bottom of the panels. Such attention to detail bodes well with buyers, who assume the sellers would take similar care with their home in general.

> lessons learned

> **DIRECT THE EYE WITH DRAMA.** The living room's custom-built bookcases give the room's prime feature—the fireplace—more selling power. Similarly a new iron chandelier draws the eye across the room to the inviting dining area. If your eyes don't gravitate to your room's key features, or there's any confusion about the purpose of a space, find a creative solution.

> **UPDATE UNDERFOOT.** Flooring is one of the first things potential home buyers notice when they walk into a room. The better it looks, the better the offers—which is why these sellers decided to replace the soiled carpet on their own. Carpet tends to be an affordable update (there's no reason to buy the most expensive pad or carpet) that leaves a good impression with buyers. If new carpeting isn't an option, have the flooring professionally cleaned. A large area rug or throw rugs also can hide less-than-perfect carpeting—just be aware that smart buyers will want to take a peek underneath the rugs.

> **SEE THE LIGHT.** Good lighting—both natural and artificial—makes a big impact. Updating light fixtures is a relatively inexpensive way to add value and style to your home; buyers will view it as one fewer thing they'll have to replace. Similarly, new window treatments can work wonders from both a style and ambiance perspective. Just make sure that window treatments don't interfere with the amount of light that comes into a room. "Letting in natural light will give a room a warm and spacious feel, and it doesn't cost a thing," *Designed to Sell* host Clive Pearse says.

> **TUNE OUT THE TV.** In everyday life positioning furniture with TV-viewing in mind is fine. Not so when you're selling your home. In this room the TV was battling the fireplace—and winning. With the TV removed, the focus is now on a feature that helps generate extra dollar signs. If you just can't live without a TV, make sure it's not the center of attention. Position furniture to capitalize on the room's best features, and be willing to sacrifice prime viewing spots or take a seat on the floor to catch your favorite shows.

> balancing act

A fireplace is a great selling point, but this large brick structure was making the living room look lopsided. With the bricks toned down with paint and furniture positioned to create a better traffic flow, the room gracefully regains its composure.

BEFORE

WHAT'S WRONG with this room? When a room is a pass-through to another area of a home, as this living room is, "it gives a bad feel to the room," real estate expert Shannon Freeman says. But all is not lost: Proper furniture placement can make such a space function better, she says. Traffic flow aside, Shannon says the biggest misstep in this room is how the furniture placement fails to draw attention to the brick fireplace. "When buyers are looking for a house, a fireplace is definitely on the list of things that they want," she says. "This is an asset to these sellers, and they really need to use this to their best advantage."

Pulling the sofa away from a wall creates a much-needed walkway behind it. The painted brick fireplace is an inviting backdrop for the new furniture arrangement.

RIGHT: It's difficult to imagine this setting as anything but calm and serene. Before the makeover the fireplace's red bricks were overbearing and unstylish. **BELOW:** Accessories, including a magazine rack placed next to a chair, help convey the message that the fireplace area is a cozy spot for relaxing.

OPPOSITE: Floor-length drapery panels cleverly camouflage the fact that the windows are actually a series of smaller ones; the panels hide the wall space between the windows. The new armoire in the corner counterbalances the wall-spanning brick fireplace on the other end of the room.

"By faux-painting the fireplace bricks, we've taken the fireplace from being too severe into a neutral color that flows with the rest of the house."
—designer Lisa LaPorta

ACTION PLAN Though the fireplace was an asset, its red hue was overwhelming and needed to be toned down—especially because the bricks spanned an entire wall. The other challenge was to improve traffic flow by repositioning furniture and do it in a way to showcase the brick wall, which made the room seem heavy at that end.

THE MAKEOVER With a red brick wall staring her in the face, interior designer Lisa LaPorta knew it would take patience and precision to tame it, working brick by brick. Not wanting the bricks to look painted—a turnoff for many buyers—she carefully dabbed on neutral-color paint with a brush and then wiped it off with a rag, allowing the red tones to show through in places for a natural look. "By faux-painting the fireplace bricks, we've taken the fireplace from being too severe into a neutral color that flows with the rest of the house," Lisa says. Walls were painted a neutral tone that complements the fireplace and allows the white-painted crown molding to pop. Furniture, including a new armoire that anchors a corner of the room opposite the fireplace, was rearranged to showcase the fireplace and at the same time create a straightforward walkway from the room's entry to the doorway at the opposite end.

> directing traffic

Homeowners may not be civil engineers, but they do need to determine the best way to direct traffic through a room. Consider these tips:

> **HALT CROSS-TRAFFIC.** No one should have to cut through a room's main area, thereby interfering with conversation or television-viewing. Pulling a sofa and chairs away from a wall into a smaller sitting area usually solves the problem by opening up a walkway behind the furnishings.

> **ELIMINATE SPEED BUMPS.** Secondary sitting or work areas should not impede across-the-room traffic. Make sure electrical cords aren't underfoot, and secure area rugs along routes with nonskid backing so a buyer doesn't end up in the emergency room.

> **KEEP LANES IN LINE.** Allow about 2½ to 3 feet for major traffic lanes. If less-busy pathways are custom-sized, such as a widened space between a sofa and a coffee table for long-legged comfort, rein those in to make the room appear larger.

> **CREATE AN ENTRY RAMP.** If your front door opens directly into the living room, create the illusion of a foyer. A decorative screen or the back of a small sofa or chair can act as a boundary.

ABOVE: Even on close inspection, the painted fireplace bricks have a natural appearance. The mantel clock plays off the tones of the bricks.

> **budget breakdown**

Armoire	$395
Accessories and plants	$97
Paint	$49
Total	$541

Fresh flowers give a room cheer, which makes them a favorite staging tool. Skip formal, fussy bouquets—which can look contrived—for more casual ones such as these roses.

RIGHT: Subtle pattern gives the room energy, without being off-putting. The striped fabric of the drapery panels visually elongates the room, yet is subtle enough to harmonize with the lamp shade's tone-on-tone pattern.
FAR RIGHT: A few dark metal accents, such as this sconce, help visually ground the room.

> lessons learned

> **GET CRAFTY.** As Lisa proved by faux-painting the fireplace bricks, there are inexpensive solutions to add value to an unappealing feature. Rather than assuming you have to gut something and start anew, look for creative updates. Decorative painting can help camouflage flaws, but consider it only for select areas that scream for help and where the result would have mass appeal. Sponge-painted walls, for example, have a limited fan base, but no one can argue that these faux-painted bricks are a big improvement over the red-hued ones.

> **CREATE A FLOW.** Most rooms have a few quirks that may foil room-arranging plans. In this case the room was a pass-through to another part of the house. With furniture placed against the walls, traffic was directed right through the space. To free up perimeter space for walkways and create a sensible traffic flow, move sofas and chairs away from walls into a tighter grouping. This also facilitates conversation and coziness.

> **MAINTAIN YOUR EQUILIBRIUM.** This room's brick wall put all the visual weight on one side of the room, creating a lopsided effect. A large armoire was positioned on the opposite wall to counterbalance the brick fireplace. Similarly new window coverings that treated a series of small windows as one larger one also helped balance the room. You don't have to match bulky elements pound for pound; just create groupings or bring in elements that add up to a comparable visual weight class.

> **USE IT OR LOSE IT.** When Shannon toured this room, a futon was taking up residence on one wall and getting in the way of walking. The sellers fessed up that the futon wasn't supposed to be there; they just hadn't gotten around to moving it out. If items in your rooms don't serve a purpose, get rid of them. Subscribe to the "use-it-or-lose-it" theory to make rooms seem larger. Sometimes you even have to lose things you use to make your home show better.

> small changes, big impact

Making a room presentable doesn't have to be a huge undertaking. With some simple furniture editing and rearranging and a few minor updates, this living room earns its keep.

BEFORE

WHAT'S WRONG with this room? Real estate expert Shannon Freeman usually has nonstop advice on how to ready a room for a sale. This living room was one of those rare exceptions. "I think this room overall looks good," she says. Regardless, every room can use a little help. Shannon's suggestions include moving the coffee table blocking the fireplace ("This is not normal," she says) and removing some of the large furnishings that are detracting from the room's spaciousness ("They're going to be moving anyway, they may as well take them out now," she says).

"Look, instant value just by moving the coffee table," host Clive Pearse notes of the piece that was used as a blockade for the fireplace. Staged with simple accessories, the coffee table is stylish in its new setting.

RIGHT: Pillows and throws are staging musts. This accent chair is made oh-so-inviting with the addition of both. For design continuity, the pillow is made from the same fabric as that used for the window treatments.

> sheen scene

Making a room shine involves more than wattage and windows. The sheen on surfaces and accessories also plays a role. As such, make sheen a part of your selling strategy.

> Paints and sealers with a glossy sheen will command attention, compared to those with no sheen. Using a glossy paint or clear sealer is an easy way to draw attention to architectural details, such as crown molding or a brick fireplace.

> Glass or silvery accessories will help bounce light around a room. Similarly mirrors and glass-top tables can visually enlarge a space. In a kitchen consider retrofitting some cabinet doors with glass or frosted-glass panels to add depth and light.

> Fabrics have different sheens and can dramatically alter a room's look. Silks and chintzes, for example, have a lustrous look. Scatter the luster about the room via pillows, or draw attention to a window with flowing panels.

ACTION PLAN Make the room buyer-friendly. The room's mix of furnishings—many of which are oversize pieces—suits the homeowners for daily living, but it makes the room feel cramped and cluttered. The coffee table blockade is another real-life ritual that had to go: The homeowners used it to keep their toddler away from the firebox. In addition to whittling the furniture, the room needs to be brighter so buyers can see what they're getting.

LEFT: A horizontal painting with layers of matting echoes the detailing of the mantel. Subtle repetition is an effective way to drive home a room's architectural elements.

THE MAKEOVER With other rooms of the house needing more attention than this one, interior designer Lisa LaPorta came up with a budget-friendly plan that would still have impact. To draw attention to the fireplace, she applied a sealant that gives the brick surround a glossy sheen. Removing shutters covering the windows lightens the room. With just a few key pieces of furniture remaining, the visual clutter is gone and the room's large size sells itself. The new furniture arrangement puts the focus on the fireplace and the view out glass doors. "This living room is a really good example of small changes making a big impact," Lisa says.

"This living room is a really good example of small changes making a big impact."
—designer Lisa LaPorta

RIGHT: An accent chair angled toward the fireplace and teamed with a floor lamp conjures images of a cozy reading space. A side chair—even one pulled from a dining set—can be used to fill an awkward corner that may otherwise stand empty.

> budget breakdown

Window treatments	$181
Accessories	$71
Brick sealant	$5
Total	$257

CHA-CHING! If you're not convinced that small changes pay off, consider this: The homeowners received three offers at the open house, and ended up selling the house for $16,000 above their asking price. (To see the kitchen makeover that also helped increase the home's value, turn to "Kitchen Resuscitation," page 112.)

RIGHT: By removing an unattractive screen clipped to the inside of the firebox, the brick surround no longer has to compete for attention. Because fireplaces are sought-after features that buyers notice, leave nothing to chance: This firebox was thoroughly vacuumed before it was staged with logs. Clean sells!

> lessons learned

> **PACK IT UP.** When you're selling your house, you'll need to load up furniture sooner or later, so make it sooner. A room that's overflowing with furniture, as this one was, makes a space seem smaller—and buyers won't pay top dollar for smaller. Even if you're not planning to sell your house anytime soon, pretend like a move is imminent so you'll be less inclined to stuff your rooms with things you really don't need or use.

> **THINK SMALL.** This room proves the point that small changes pay off. If a room seems "done" to you, find a way to make it even better—say with new throw pillows that add a splash of color. If a room seems too overwhelming to tackle, start with updates that provide instant gratification, such as rearranging furniture or painting the walls.

> **RETHINK THE CHILD-PROOFING.** It's understandable that sellers who have toddlers want their rooms to be safe, but a house that's for sale needs to cater to adults. That means no coffee table blocking the fireplace, as was the case in this room. If you must have furnishings or accessories placed a certain way for safety reasons, allot an extra hour before the open house to stage things so they appeal to the mortgage-paying public, not babies.

> **LIGHTEN THE LOAD.** Lisa had a quick tip for the *Designed to Sell* team as it moved the sofa around: Remove the cushions and pillows. Indeed those seemingly innocent extras can add back-straining bulk. Similarly if you're having trouble getting a sofa or chair to fit through a doorway or down a narrow corridor, check the legs: Some can be unscrewed to allow a critical bit of leeway.

> side by side

Front doors that usher people directly into a room or spaces that flow into one another can be selling challenges. Color and a defined style help link these adjacent rooms, increasing the value in the process.

BEFORE

WHAT'S WRONG with this room? There was good reason why real estate expert Shannon Freeman was underwhelmed when she stepped through this home's front door and saw a room that was essentially a vast wasteland, except for a few toys and some exercise equipment. "I don't know what it is," she says. "Is it a foyer? An exercise room? When buyers are purchasing a house based on square footage, how can you justify this in your sale price?" The mystery room flowed into the living room, which was crowded with furniture and featured a faux-painted fireplace. "Having a fireplace is a good thing, but this finish is very, very taste-specific," Shannon says of the spotted design, "which is something to avoid when your house is on the market because you have many different people coming through your home with many different tastes." As would be expected from a keen-eyed agent, the smaller shortcomings added up to big missteps too: A wobbly, dated railing in the entry room, and a front door with peeling paint and a missing knob didn't make a good first impression. "If you're going to buy a house, you deserve a doorknob," Shannon says.

This L-shape furniture grouping helps create a walkway so the living room's traffic flow isn't through the center of the room. The television that everything formerly centered around is gone.

> "By painting [the fireplace] this rich burgundy color, it really just makes it look like a rich, lovely focal point."
> —*designer Lisa LaPorta*

ACTION PLAN Go with the flow. Because the two rooms were connected via a wide open doorway, they begged for continuity. The empty entry room needed an identity that would mesh with the living room. The dated railing in the entry room was removed to open up the space, and the front door that ushered people into the room received new paint and hardware.

ABOVE: Deep burgundy paint gives the fireplace bricks a rich look. Though natural bricks tend to have more selling power than painted ones, this fireplace was an exception because the bricks already had been faux-painted. Lisa used a chip brush to paint the bricks; the natural hog-bristle brushes are inexpensive enough to discard after being used.

ABOVE: New window treatments frame the view and accentuate the generous window size. **LEFT:** Matching chairs face the dining room to give buyers an inviting focal point when they enter the living room. The grouping also draws the eye toward the fireplace. Lisa created two seating areas to make sense of the room's awkward shape.

THE MAKEOVER Interior designer Lisa LaPorta devised a scheme to ensure that each space gave buyers a grand entrance. The plan started at the front door: "A front door that's in bad shape would be a real red flag to potential home buyers," she says. The door was sanded and painted, and new hardware was added. The wobbly railing just inside the door was removed to open up the room. To give the empty space value, Lisa turned it into a dining area. In the living room she painted over the faux-painted brick fireplace. "By painting it this rich burgundy color, it really just makes it look like a rich, lovely focal point of the room and it really adds value," Lisa says. With a substantial entertainment center removed from the room and the furniture rearranged into two inviting seating areas, the living room's size and features stood out. A neutral color scheme links the living room with the newly defined dining area.

> in focus

When a room has an awkward shape or it just doesn't feel right for some reason, step back and assess the situation. If something seems off to you, you can bet it will to buyers too. Consider these tips:

> **FIND THE FOCAL POINT.** Is a big entertainment center overshadowing your room? Often extraneous items get in the way of a room's focal point, the all-important cornerstone that furnishings should be placed around. A fireplace, a great view, or a wall of built-ins are possible building blocks for a thoughtful furniture arrangement. You also can get creative, grouping furnishings around a painting or freestanding shelves; just make sure the new focal point deserves the attention.

> **DO THE MATH.** Often you have to subtract to add value. Could you create floor space by removing some furnishings? Would a lifeless room seem more inviting if you divided it into sitting areas or activity centers?

> **BREAK THE RULES.** Who says a sofa must be paired with a coffee table? Try bringing in a slim bench to add character and give the illusion of more floor space. Remember, selling a home is about creating an inviting ambiance and showing off square footage.

> budget breakdown

Furniture $481

Door hardware, paint, & supplies $240

Lamps & accessories $234

Window treatments $175

Living room paint and supplies $20

Total $1,150

CHA-CHING! Confident because of the improvements in these two key rooms, these homeowners rejected initial offers from buyers. Three weeks after the open house, they had an offer for $5,000 above their asking price. (See "Regaining A Garage," page 170, to see how the *Designed to Sell* team transformed what's often a neglected space.)

RIGHT: To create a more open floor plan and seamless flow, the *Designed to Sell* team rearranged furniture and removed a wobbly iron railing in the front entrance. The railing had visually diminished the size of what is now the dining room. The front door also received a much-needed facelift with a new coat of paint and new hardware.

> lessons learned

> **CREATE VISUAL VALUE.** This 1,590-square-foot home wasn't used to its full potential until Lisa defined a basically empty room off the front entrance as a dining room. "You can charge an awful lot of money for having a dining room," Lisa says. "We are showing buyers that it's valuable, useful space worth spending money on." It's the same house and same square footage, but it seems bigger. Remember that every square foot of space counts, and it's up to you to show the value of it.

> **WARM UP THE WELCOME.** When sprucing up a home, don't overlook the first thing buyers pass through: the front door. "An inviting front door is the first step in pulling buyers in and pulling in the offers," host Clive Pearse says. Though the door to this home had an interesting arch shape, its gray-blue paint was peeling and didn't command much attention. Sanded, painted a deep brick color, and outfitted with new hardware, the door is an eye-catching and welcoming passageway into the home.

> **FORGO THE FAUX.** Like a favorite food or color, decorative paint treatments are highly personal. There's no place for them when you're selling your home. The faux treatment on this brick fireplace had limited appeal that would cause buyers to ponder how they could fix the problem. As with everything there are exceptions to the no-faux rule; some decorative paint treatments can help tone down an off-putting feature. (See "Balancing Act," page 44, to see how Lisa used a decorative paint treatment to tone down a red brick fireplace.)

> **DO SOME LIGHT DEMO.** You may be amazed how just a little bit of demolition can transform a space. Removing the dated iron railing in the front room of this home instantly transported the room out of the '70s. The same goes for other decorative elements that may be keeping your house from stepping into the modern world. Removing a scalloped wooden valance attached to kitchen cabinets or an ornate scroll design on a built-in bookcase rank among those "Why didn't I do that sooner?" projects. The more you can do to rid your home of elements that date it (shag carpeting and avocado green appliances included), the more buyers will be willing to pay for it.

TOP: The mere presence of a dining set gives this front-entry room a clear identity. At $406 the table and chairs were a bargain—partially due to the fact the *Designed to Sell* team assembled them. "If you're not afraid of hard work, you can save money by putting furniture together yourself," Lisa says. **LEFT:** A few punches of red enliven the neutral scheme. To appeal to the most buyers, Lisa saved the colorful touches for easy-to-change accessories.

> making sense of space

Clean lines and smart furniture placement help these two spaces—one large, the other small—maximize their potential.

BEFORE

WHAT'S WRONG with this room? Real estate expert Donna Freeman knew exactly where the homeowners went awry. "They've done *everything* wrong in here," she says. Furniture grouped at one end made the spacious living room look lopsided, and worse, only half its size. Though the adjoining dining room was small, a tiny table with mismatched chairs only played in to the size issue and gave the room a sort of childlike eat-and-run feel. "This is a formal dining room, but it looks like a formal snack room," Donna says. Both spaces had an unfinished feel, right down to the window treatments that looked like sarongs attached to rods and left Donna wondering if the sellers had flunked window-treatment class. "Do the buyers' work for them," she advises. "Make them walk in and go 'Yeah, I want to pay more for this house.'"

Walls painted a pale golden tone lend continuity between the living room and dining room. By keeping things simple—even the wood floors are without throw rugs—the room has a clean, airy look.

Spreading furnishings across the living room emphasizes the large size of the space. Chairs face off with the sofa, rather than the television behind them, to create a welcoming sitting area and kick the room into selling mode.

ACTION PLAN

Use every inch. Though the size challenges are different in the two rooms, both spaces need to maximize their square footage. New window treatments, paint, and accessories also will help warm up the visually cold, stark spaces.

"Do the buyers' work for them. Make them walk in and go 'Yeah, I want to pay more for this house.'"

—real estate expert
Donna Freeman

RIGHT: To stretch your decorating dollars, look for new uses for existing items. Lisa grouped four wooden cubes to form a large coffee table that anchors the conversation area. The cubes were aligned under a window to create a bench.

TOP: Hung near the ceiling, the patterned valance heightens the room's sense of spaciousness. "An important aspect of hanging a valance or cornice is to leave a little bit of paint line showing," Lisa says. "If you go to the ceiling, it does funny things in terms of chopping up the room."

ABOVE: A glass vase and wooden bowl offer shapely contrast to the grid design of the accent tables.

THE MAKEOVER

Knowing that a large space can be both a blessing and a curse, interior designer Lisa LaPorta set out to cozy up the living room while still showing off its size. She positioned furniture to fill the length of the room; the savvy arrangement groups a colorful new sofa and chairs into a conversation area. New window treatments consisting of a tailored valance and flowing panels provide visual warmth and draw the eye upward to accentuate the high ceiling. "The valances really give an architectural detail to the windows to sort of compete with all this volume," Lisa says. Despite the dining room's small size, Lisa felt a large—or at least standard-size table—was needed to stage the room as a high-functioning space. With the homeowners deciding to purchase a new dining set, the team's budget was freed up a bit for new window treatments and a few accessories. Deep red drapery panels and accessories help the dining room make a splash; similar color accents in the living room visually connect the two spaces.

> it's all in the details

When you're done with the painting, take a few minutes to organize partially used quarts and gallons. Interior designer Lisa LaPorta suggests clearly labeling paint cans, noting which room or rooms the paint was used in, and leaving the cans in a tidy row on a garage or basement shelf. "It's a really nice touch that shows buyers your attention to detail," she says. Buyers will appreciate having the paint for touch-ups, and the labeling implies that you've taken similar care with the house in general.

A new dining set that fits the scale of the space gives this formerly bland dining room a modern and more adultlike look. Deep red accessories add an extra bit of energy to engage buyers, yet they don't have the permanency that may scare color-shy house hunters away.

CHA-CHING! Just one day after the open house, the sellers accepted an offer for $5,000 above their original asking price—money they planned to put to good use to help build their dream home in the mountains. See "The Little Kitchen That Could," page 100, and "From All White To Just Right," page 156, to see how the *Designed to Sell* team remade other rooms in the house.

>budget breakdown

Furniture	$483
Window treatments	$335
Accessories	$195
Paint & Supplies	$60
Total	$1,073

RIGHT: Shelves hung in a staggered formation echo the contours of the pitched ceiling, and stylishly fill an awkward empty space created by moving the sofa away from the wall. Painted the same color as the wall, the shelves visually recede and seem almost like an architectural element. **FAR RIGHT:** Grommeted drapery panels slipped onto a slim silvery rod give the dining room a modern edge, but not so contemporary that it compromises the goal of having mass appeal.

> lessons learned

> **DON'T GIVE AN INCH.** Short of building on, you can't change your home's square footage. But you can visually alter it. Though this dining room was small, bringing in a larger dining set—something that sounds contrary to reason—made the room seem like a highly functional space, hence more square footage. The key is to maximize square footage without crowding a room—something that may take several attempts.

> **SIMPLICITY SELLS.** Giving your spaces breathing room creates a visually clean and more airy look—which translates into more space in a buyer's mind. In addition to keeping furnishings to a minimum,

resist the urge to over- decorate. Think solid colors (pattern—at least large expanses of it—can make a room seem busy). Limit artwork to just a few well-chosen pieces. In both of these rooms, clean-line furnishings also contribute to the stylish simplicity.

> **ADD SPLASHES OF COLOR.** Though you may have "neutral" etched into your brain, there's still a place for color when showing your home. Color gives dull rooms a burst of energy. Buyers may not like the particular hue you've chosen, but they'll like the vibe they get from the room. As Lisa did in these rooms, save the bold hues for accessories and furnishings.

A bright blue sofa is more forgiving to color-timid buyers than is a bright blue wall that they'll have to paint over.

> **STAGE FOR PROFITS.** If there's one thing the *Designed to Sell* team preaches, it's that you have to make sacrifices in daily living to reap the biggest reward in selling. In this living room, for example, the new furniture arrangement wasn't as conducive as it could be for watching TV. It was, however, the best way to show off the room's spaciousness while still making it seem cozy. What's more important to you: being a couch potato or pocketing more money when you sell your house? It's your call.

> four-star retreat

This dark and style-deprived space had all the charm of a cheap hotel room. Brightened and modernized, it now rates as an inviting retreat.

BEFORE

WHAT'S WRONG with this room? With green carpeting, sofas upholstered in a printed fabric, and sheers covering the windows, this dark living/dining room seemed oddly familiar to real estate expert Shannon Freeman. "It reminds me of a two-star hotel room," she says. Though there was nothing cheap-looking about the marble fireplace surround, the fireplace lacked a mantelpiece that would give it presence. It was also lost in a throng of furniture. "The fireplace is just going by the wayside," Shannon says. Swatches of three different paint colors brushed onto one wall were reminders of a project the homeowners never completed—and a big question mark to buyers about what else the owners may have neglected. From the front door to her first steps inside, Shannon also noticed that there was nothing striking or unique to set this townhouse apart from the others: "Why should someone buy this house instead of the next seven down the way?" she asks.

Never underestimate the power of natural light. New drapery panels are pulled to the sides of the windows to usher in sunlight. The glass-top coffee table that anchors the sitting area is another light-enhancing addition. Though large in size, it's visually light.

ACTION PLAN Raise the two-star rating. New furniture, carpeting, and window treatments are needed to make the space seem more like a home than a hotel—and to brighten and modernize it. The fireplace must command more attention, and the furniture should be repositioned to showcase this feature. Stark white walls need to be painted to warm up the room.

"It reminds me of a two-star hotel room."
—real estate expert Shannon Freeman

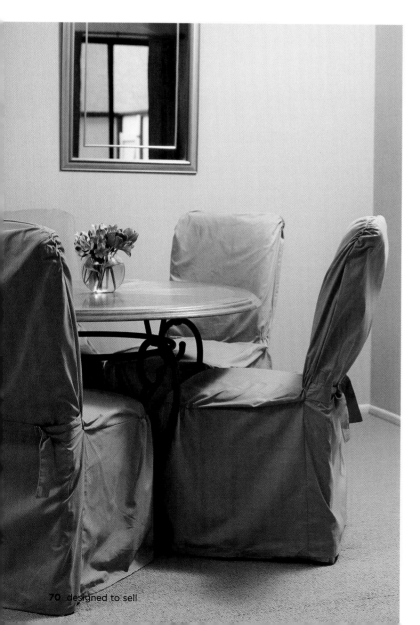

LEFT: A mirror reflects the view out one of the living room windows and gives the illusion that there's a window on this side of the dining area. **TOP:** If fixtures are a home's "jewelry," then this chandelier is a gem compared to the dated brassy fixture it replaced. **ABOVE:** Framed and matted color photos bring the room into bloom and can be an affordable way to fill empty wall space. Other inexpensive options for artwork include vintage or new calendars and posters from local festivals.

THE MAKEOVER Knowing that this home would need to make a dramatic first impression to set it apart from other units, the *Designed to Sell* team earmarked more than half of its $2,000 budget for the two rooms. A mantelpiece built with less than $70 worth of materials helps the fireplace gain focal-point status. New window treatments are another inexpensive change—just slightly more than $100—that dramatically transform the space by making it brighter and more modern. A smart blend of new furniture and carefully culled existing items also brings the rooms into the 2000s. Even though the team brought one of the patterned sofas back into the living room, neutral furnishings, a warmer wall color, and the beige carpet the homeowners purchased help tone down the busy pattern.

> mirror mirror

Mirrors are a great way to visually expand a space, but in the wrong hands the results can be counterproductive. Homeowners need to think less about what the frames look like and more about what the mirrors will reflect. So before you pound any nails in the wall, check out the reflection. Buyers should see something appealing from every vantage point—even when they look in a mirror. If the image staring back at you from a mirror doesn't add value, find something else to hang there.

ABOVE: This accent chair, which angles toward the fireplace area, is a visually lighter alternative to a recliner or other upholstered chair. Lisa whittled down the bevy of furniture to a few well-chosen items, and brought in a few new pieces that worked better with the space.

> budget breakdown

Furniture $460

Dining set $267

Chandelier $195

Window treatments $103

Accessories $78

Mantel lumber
& materials $67

Paint and supplies $50

Total $1,220

CHA-CHING! The home sellers' real estate agent could almost smell the money on this one. The improvements to the living/dining room (as well as the master bedroom, see "Playing Up the Positive," page 144, and bathroom, see "Bathing Beauty," page 130) were so impressive she encouraged the homeowners to substantially increase their asking price. One week and four offers later, they ended up with $23,000 above their original asking price.

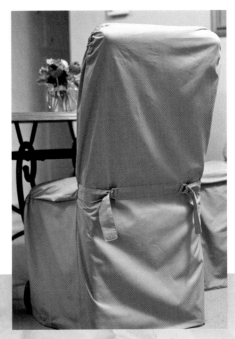

OPPOSITE: Outfitted with a new mantelpiece, the fireplace is now the star of the living room. The walls are painted a warm hue that contrasts with the white mantelpiece. **RIGHT:** A sculptural metal piece replaced a mirror that hung above the fireplace and reflected an unimpressive view of the side of the staircase. **FAR RIGHT:** Slipcovers on the dining chairs blend with the new carpeting and wall color for a cohesive look. Slipcovers can camouflage dated or dirty furniture and visually soften wooden or metal pieces.

> lessons learned

> **MODERNIZE FOR MONEY.** Decorating trends come and go and, granted, it can be expensive to stay in tune with the times. But buyers are smitten by cosmetics and they want a home that seems "happening." Even if you've updated your electrical system and put on a new roof, rooms flowing with the jewel tones of the '90s (as this room was), the mauves of the '80s, or other decades-ago color schemes is a profit-impeding turnoff.

> **SHOW SOME SHEER WILL.** Real estate expert Shannon Freeman has some simple advice for home sellers and their window treatments: "Take down your sheers and fatten up the pocketbook," she says. The dated sheers on the windows of this living room may have served a purpose at some point, but from a selling strategy they made the room seem dark. Removing drapery panels also can make a room seem larger by opening the space to the outdoors. If privacy is an issue, purchase inexpensive paper shades that are designed for temporary use. The shades, which are available at many stores that sell window treatments, tape onto the window trim, and can be easily removed before an open house.

> **TONE IT DOWN.** Because color and pattern are matters of personal taste, they're best reserved for easy-to-change items. These homeowners learned that lesson when they paid to replace the green carpeting in their living/dining room with neutral color carpet.

Their patterned sofas also made the room feel busy. When you're getting ready to sell, think solid-color fabrics and neutral surfaces. Save the pattern and color for throw pillows or artwork.

> **DON'T REST ON YOUR LAURELS.** Touting a home's high-end touches—such as a marble fireplace or granite countertops—on a sell sheet is a great way to pique buyers' interest. But if you raise expectations, you better deliver. If buyers had seen this room's fireplace before the makeover, they may have felt they were getting shortchanged: a nice marble surround, but no mantelpiece. Even great features can be made better, justifying a higher asking price.

> open to change

A new window and splashes of bright color give a bleak living room a bright new future with selling potential.

BEFORE

WHAT'S WRONG with this room? Real estate expert Donna Freeman has been in enough dark houses—this living room included—to know the gloomy prospect of getting top dollar. "I don't know how anyone can make an offer on a house if they need a floodlight to see it," she says. Faux-finished walls had just enough detail to make buyers wonder if the homeowners were trying to hide flaws. In addition to being dark, the room lacked pizzazz. There was nothing compelling to make Donna—or buyers—spend any time in there, and that went against one of her selling principles. "I like for a potential buyer to spend as much time as they can in a room so they can get the feel of it," she says.

The once dark living room is now light and airy, thanks to the new window added on the wall with the sectional.

Filling a room with a large sectional usually isn't a good idea when selling a home, but this living room is able to accommodate the size. Positioned below the new window, the sectional draws attention to the feature.

"I like for a potential buyer to spend as much time as they can in a room so they can get the feel of it."

—real estate expert Donna Freeman

 **ACTION PLAN** Give buyers reasons to stick around. Add a new window to let in light. Replace the futon and other style-challenged furniture with comfy new pieces. Bring in color and visual intrigue through accessories and window treatments.

Candles are an easy way to bring color into a room, as these ones do. Another bonus is that this grouping draws the eye to the wood floor.

THE MAKEOVER Interior designer Lisa LaPorta tapped the skills of the *Designed to Sell* contractors—and a homeowner eager to wield a sledgehammer—to install a new window that lifts the room from the dark ages. Adding that window was a $306 investment that added thousands of dollars to the value of the home. Painting over the faux-finish walls created a clean canvas for new furnishings. A sectional sofa takes the place of a grouping of smaller furnishings, and offers sink-in appeal that the other pieces lacked. Positioning one section under the new window created a focal point on the far side of the room. Splashes of rusty red and gold in the window treatments, an area rug, and accessories add intrigue—a must to keep buyers from rushing on through.

> working with windows

A new window may be out of your budget, but there are ways to visually improve the windows you have. For starters, remove the screens (weather permitting). Screens reduce the amount of light coming into a room and detract from what you see out the window. The extra brightness may make you feel like you've gained an entirely new window. Wooden insets can be inserted easily into the interior frame of casement windows to mimic the look of paned ones. New molding can give a lackluster window more prominence, as can painting the frame around the window. Black-painted frames, for example, command attention, drawing the eye outdoors and visually expanding the room. On the exterior, window boxes and new shutters (or at least newly painted ones) can jazz up the look.

> budget breakdown

Furniture	$650
Window and supplies	$306
Window treatments	$91
Accessories	$57
Total	$1,104

RIGHT: Flickering candles cast a warm glow against the brick fireplace. If candles are lit when showing a home, make sure an adult is nearby to keep a close watch on them.

CHA-CHING! The revamped living room, as well as the adjoining dining room (see "Dining By Design," page 92), wowed buyers from the moment they walked in the door. Seven offers rolled in, and the homeowners sold their house for $26,000 above their asking price. See "Ready For Guests," page 150, for the other makeover in this house.

> lessons learned

> **SQUEEGEE SOME STYLE.** Washing windows is no one's favorite chore, but windows should sparkle inside and out. It's not just the glass that needs your attention: The trim and sills must be spiffy, and latches and turning mechanisms should be in working order. Replace damaged screens. If you're removing screens for staging purposes, keep them handy so serious buyers can check them out.

> **GRAB THEIR ATTENTION.** You don't want buyers rushing out of a room, as Donna wanted to do here. Dramatic touches compel them to stay. Lisa brought this dull living room to life with pops of reddish orange and gold. Even the beige sectional sofa has a "wow" factor: Buyers can imagine themselves sinking into the comfy cushions. It's an inviting alternative to the futon that formerly sat there.

> **KEEP IT CLEAN.** Of course your home should be spotless when you show it. But visual clutter drags a selling price down faster than dusty tabletops. Simplify your decor by scaling back. It's often better to stage a room with just a few large pieces than with a series of small ones, which can be distracting.

> **SIZE UP THE VIEW.** Whether you're adding a new window or dealing with existing ones, what you see out them can influence buyers. A window that looks onto a flower garden stirs a different emotion than one that looks onto the neighbor's trash cans. If you have a bad view, block it or camouflage it with window treatments. Even a small valance can work wonders by partially blocking or at least distracting buyers from the problem spot.

Lisa chose an earthy palette to complement the hues of the brick chimney. Colorful accessories on the mantel pick up the red tones in the brick.

> aging gracefully

This room had the charm of a dorm room or first apartment until the *Designed to Sell* team gave it grown-up style with buyer appeal.

BEFORE

WHAT'S WRONG with this room? Though she was impressed with the exterior of this 1952 home, real estate expert Shannon Freeman's high hopes for the interior were dashed when she stepped through the front door into the living/dining room. "It was suburban heaven on the outside and now I've walked into a college dormitory," she says. "This seems so temporary to me." Shabby furniture, a cheap-looking chandelier, and dreary wood paneling contributed to the makeshift and dated look. A fish tank placed in front of the fireplace further detracted from the value. "These sellers are literally taking money out of their pocket by not showing off this fantastic feature," Shannon says.

Lisa grouped the new furnishings into a cozy sitting area centered on the fireplace a contrast to the previous arrangement that had furniture backed against the walls leaving an empty, wasted spot in the middle of the room.

Simple updates, such as painting the walls and hanging valances on the windows, give the dining/living room a stylish shell for buyers to build upon.

> easy does it

When a project requires light demolition, such as removing a mantel from a fireplace, be gentle. You'll save time and money in the long run by minimizing repairs needed to the drywall or other surfaces damaged in the process. Use the proper tools, and protect floors and nearby surfaces with drop cloths.

ACTION PLAN Graduate the style. Shannon's critique involved words such as "dormitory," "college furniture," and "apartment"—not exactly flattering descriptions for home buyers to hear or to see. New furniture, paint, and a fireplace mantel will freshen the room and give it a style update to appeal to buyers who have more discriminating tastes.

RIGHT: Flourishes, such as a stack of books on the coffee table and candles in the firebox, complete the look of the living room.

THE MAKEOVER Interior designer Lisa LaPorta started the transformation as she does most of her rooms: with paint. A pale earthy hue refreshed the walls, including the dark, dated paneling on the fireplace wall and the lower walls of the dining room. To draw attention to the fireplace, the team replaced the mantel, which was nothing more than a plank of wood, with a more substantial and detailed piece. In the dining room, a new chandelier brings a modern touch up high, as do colorful valances on the welcoming series of windows along the back wall of both spaces. Stylish new furniture proportioned to the rooms completes the look; in the living room, furniture is moved away from the walls to form a more centrally located sitting area near the fireplace.

> "It was suburban heaven on the outside and now I've walked into a college dormitory."
>
> —real estate expert Shannon Freeman

Streamlining is the name of the game when cashing in on a house. A wall that once was cluttered with electronics and framed photos now has plenty of breathing room.

Painting the paneled wall in a light neutral tone lifted the room from the dark ages and put the focus on the fireplace.

ABOVE: The new mantel's detailing and wider, deeper size give the fireplace added prominence. The previous mantel was a straight piece of wood; it had the same reddish tones as the paneling and it disappeared into the wall.

Replacing the cheap-looking brassy light fixture with this graciously curved one gives the dining room a boost in value. The new dining set is not only better proportioned for the room, its darker wood tone helps anchor the setting.

> budget breakdown

Furniture	$663
Lighting	$111
Mantel	$107
Accessories	$69
Paint and supplies	$50
Window treatments	$22
Total	$1,022

CHA-CHING! With 16 offers in three days, these homeowners were in a good place—in a bidding war that enabled them to sell their house for $26,000 above the asking price. See "Luxury Despite Limitations," page 124, to view the other transformation in this home.

BELOW: The lower walls sport a deeper hue than the upper walls. When painting a two-tone treatment, use the darker color on the bottom to prevent a top-heavy look. **RIGHT:** Candles give the shelves a color boost.

> lessons learned

> **MAKE IT A HOME.** These sellers knew their furnishings gave the home a temporary feel. They were fine with that because they didn't envision the house as being permanent for them, and they didn't want to invest in more stylish items. Buyers, though, want a house they can imagine settling in for the long haul. Make your home warm and inviting, and give it a sense of permanency with furnishings scaled to the rooms, not to your previous apartment.

> **FLAUNT THE FIREPLACE.** A fireplace adds value, so put yours out there in full view (read that this way: no fish tank blocking it). Place furniture and accessories to draw the eye to the fireplace. If your fireplace is dated or downright ugly, find creative ways to make it more appealing. Adding a new mantel or painting the bricks can dramatically change the look.

> **LEAVE THE PAST BEHIND.** Remnants of a bygone era drag down the selling price of a house, as the dark paneling and brassy light fixture did in this home. Take a tour of your home to make sure it's not in a time warp. Harvest gold appliances are an obvious throwback, but so are smaller things like almond-color switch plates with dirty toggle switches. Even those small things send a signal to buyers that the home isn't new, and therefore not worthy of the asking price. Update as much as you can; camouflage what you can't.

> **MATCH THE BOOK TO ITS COVER.** Making your home look good from the outside is key to getting buyers inside, but don't disappoint them as this house did Shannon. The first rooms buyers see are critical. If the only "wow" room is your master suite on the second floor, buyers may not stick around long enough to see it. Trace the steps a house hunter would take, and make sure the journey starts with a bang.

> all the right moves

Stuffed to the brim, this multitasking space was frenetic and difficult to navigate. Now, it's an easygoing shadow of its former self.

BEFORE

WHAT'S WRONG with this room? Real estate expert Shannon Freeman encountered a first in this combination living room/dining room when she spotted a portable toilet. Though it was still in its box—one of many that caused the eye to skip past the great fireplace—she knew its presence would flush away money. The same went for the plethora of personal belongings that were better off in storage. "When your house is on the market those precious things have a place they need to be, and this is not the place," she says. Similarly a huge table was overtaking the dining area. In both spaces the inefficiency was simply a deal breaker, Shannon says. "It's not set up correctly. It's not set up to be on the market and it's not using the space efficiently."

The look is light and airy in this combination living room/dining room, thanks to a major decluttering and the addition of simple clean-line furnishings and accessories. Area rugs define the two spaces but are small enough to keep the wood floors prominent.

Get rid of excess. To remake what Shannon described as a thrift store, the boxes and excessive personal belongings need to be moved to a storage area. New paint, furnishings, and window treatments will give the room both a visually and physically cleaner look.

Breezy window treatments provide a whisper of color and contrast with the white window trim and paned windows. Windows flanking the fireplace are dressed with just one panel—hung on the outer edge. The look gives these three elements a sense of grandeur by making them seem as one continuous unit. The budget-savvy strategy also requires one fewer pair of panels.

ABOVE: Once lost in a sea of clutter and furnishings, the fireplace is now the room's selling point. Sandy beige walls provide just enough contrast to let the white mantelpiece pop. On the coffee table, a basket of lemons provides a zesty color punch that helps direct the eye toward the fireplace.

"Is this someone's living room or have I just wandered into a thrift store?"

—*real estate expert Shannon Freeman*

THE MAKEOVER For interior designer Lisa LaPorta, proper furniture placement is key to every room's success. With that in mind, she transformed this living area by situating two sofas toward the center of the room to accentuate the fireplace and create a pathway at the perimeter. The newly established pathway flows into the dining area, where a small round table makes the space equally easy to navigate. Sandy beige walls and window treatments create a serene backdrop and just enough contrast to allow the white trim and panes on the windows to stand out. Visually light accessories, including shapely vases with wispy bouquets of dried grasses, further the sense of spaciousness and newfound function.

BELOW LEFT: This window treatment offers a lesson in how to properly hang tab-top panels. The rod is installed several inches above the window trim so the top of the panel hits right at the trim. **BELOW MIDDLE:** Placing candles in a firebox, as Lisa did here, is a quick way to stage what would otherwise be an uninteresting black hole. **BELOW RIGHT:** An earthy bouquet and a picture propped against the wall create a simple yet sculptural vignette.

> bit by bit

It's common to see the *Designed to Sell* team hunkered over a box of unassembled furniture. Putting furniture together yourself usually reduces the purchase price. The downside is that it can be time-consuming and frustrating. For example, driving screws into a hexagonal socket using a flimsy allen wrench that comes in the box, can be awkward and inefficient. If you don't have sturdier tools to fall back on, clip off the wrench's handle to turn the remaining portion into a drill bit, and then use a drill to power the screws into place.

Large furnishings are placed in one continuous line—the sofas face off behind the dining table—creating an easy flow that continues right through the large window at the far end of the room. **LEFT:** The clean lines of this console table and accessories echo the room's simple style; the display visually balances the mantel on the opposite wall.

> budget breakdown

Furniture	$995
Lighting and accessories	$125
Window treatments	$53
Paint and supplies	$50
Total	$1,223

CHA-CHING! The restyled living and dining room was such an improvement that the confident sellers decided to raise their asking price by $20,000—a sizeable margin considering the *Designed to Sell* team spent just $1,223 to transform the two spaces.

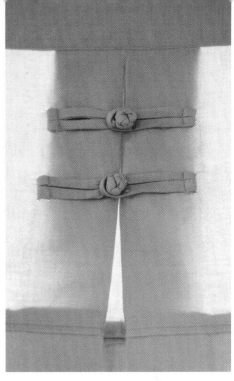

ABOVE: For $20, these valances were money well spent. They finish off the French doors in the dining room, yet are sheer enough to not command too much attention or block light. **RIGHT:** A mirror in the dining room is strategically hung to reflect the living room's key features: the fireplace and paned windows. **FAR RIGHT:** Detailing on the valances, which is echoed on the panels on the living room window, adds a designer look. Small details appeal to buyers, who are looking for signs that a home has been lovingly tended to.

> lessons learned

> **LET IT FLOW.** Even though your home's floor plan is new to house hunters, they should be able to get from Point A to Point B easily. Rearrange furnishings to create an easy flow and maximize square footage. For Lisa this usually means moving sofas and chairs away from walls to eliminate wasted space in the middle of a room.

> **PACK IT UP.** Jump-start your move by boxing belongings before buyers have a chance to rule out your house as too small. Clutter and excessive knickknacks and personal belongings make even a large room, as this one was, seem cramped. You'll gain valuable square footage and you'll have much of your work done when moving day crunch time rolls around.

> **CONNECT THE DOTS.** It's always a good idea to create continuity between rooms, especially in the public areas. Color is usually the easiest way to connect different spaces. The pale beige that dominates this combination living/dining room coordinates with a golden hue in the kitchen, which is visible through the dining room door. Bedrooms and other personal spaces offer more leeway as to how you stage and decorate because they're usually set apart from other rooms.

> **USE NATURE'S BOUNTY.** Though fresh flowers should be a part of every home seller's staging strategy, they're not the only option. Lisa put foliage—seen as weeds to many people—to effective use to create artful bouquets on the mantel and dining room table. The earthy hues and texture provide visual interest, and the wispy style fits the room's airy look. Scour your backyard or ditches for goods for these no-cost bouquets.

> dining by design

Thanks to streamlining and styling, a space barely recognizable as a dining room has a clear identity and a fresh new look.

BEFORE

WHAT'S WRONG with this room? The last thing a seller wants is a big question mark associated with the first room buyers see. "Exactly what room is this?" asks real estate expert Donna Freeman after stepping through the front door. "If I'm asking this, I know a buyer will ask too." The answer: A dining room—and a poorly defined one at that. A small table with benches was positioned toward the back of the room and not visible from the entry; a plaid tablecloth and area rug conjured images of a picnic. Most visible were the items that have the least buyer appeal—a small television and a microwave oven and toaster oven that spilled out from the adjoining kitchen. Overhead, a hodgepodge of lights—two different ceiling fans and a light fixture—were oddly placed from a functional standpoint. "It's nice square footage, it's just not put to good use," Donna says.

Staging the space with a large dining table that's visible upon entering the home gives the dining room a clear identity. The old table is positioned parallel to the window at the back of the room.

A slim green cabinet pops against a brick wall, making a simple yet striking statement. Lisa "borrowed" the cabinet from another room of the house— a no-cost way to stage a room. If need be, borrow from neighbors or friends.

"Exactly what room is this? If I'm asking this, I know a buyer will ask too."

—*real estate expert Donna Freeman*

ACTION PLAN Find the focus. A new furniture arrangement with a table prominently positioned is needed so buyers make an immediate connection to the room's purpose. Removing the clutter on the wall buyers first see will make the room seem larger and cleaner. Overhead lighting needs to be streamlined and positioned in more sensible locations.

THE MAKEOVER Giving the room a clear identity was at the top of interior designer Lisa LaPorta's list, but it wasn't the only thing driving her design. Because the dining room was the first space visible upon entering the house, she also wanted it to set the tone for what was to come. A clean, streamlined look and earthy palette that complements the exterior colors achieve that. A brick wall that was almost a straight shot from the front door was staged with a colorful cabinet—and nothing more. Minus the clutter, the wall is now a texturally intriguing focal point. A larger table and chairs centered in the room leave no doubt that the space is designed for dining. Taking the streamlined look to the ceiling, the *Designed to Sell* team replaced a mismatched trio of lighting with four recessed lights and a modern pendent light centered above the table. New drapery panels and slipcovers on the backs of the chairs at a breakfast bar soften the look and introduce the earthy reddish-brown hue that's woven throughout the house. The updates turned the misguided room into valuable square footage—exactly what Donna hoped for.

ABOVE LEFT: Slipcovers dress up the chairs at the breakfast bar. Staging the counter with place mats and fresh flowers also helps the setting segue from the hardworking kitchen on the other side of the bar to an inviting dining room. **ABOVE RIGHT:** This curvy candleholder that hangs on a wall in the entry echoes the curves of the new light fixture above the dining table.

> illuminating ideas

You may have been taught to turn off the lights when you leave a room, but when you show your home do the opposite to make it shine. To be most effective, rooms need a blend of general, task, and accent lighting. For example:

> General lighting, also called ambient lighting, is the overall lighting. Ceiling-mounted fixtures and chandeliers fall into this category. As a general rule, provide at least 1,700 lumens (the light output generated by a 100-watt incandescent bulb or a 25-watt fluorescent bulb) for each 50 square feet of floor space.

> Task lighting illuminates a specific area, such as a bathroom mirror or kitchen island. Pendent lights or recessed lights offer task lighting. If your bathroom has "Hollywood makeup table" lighting—round bulbs mounted to a strip—splurge on a new fixture. They are outdated and cast a garish glow.

> Accent lighting is designed to showcase a specific item, such as artwork, or to simply give a room a bit of extra sparkle. Wall sconces, recessed uplights, and even a row of lit candles can provide this warm glow.

CHA-CHING! Serving up style in this dining room paid off for these homeowners. Seven days and seven offers after the open house, they sold their house for $26,000 above the asking price. Transforming the living room (see "Open to Change," page 74) and bedroom (see "Ready For Guests," page 150) also parlayed into a big payback.

> budget
breakdown

Lighting $175

Window treatments $69

Paint and supplies $31

Stool covers $11

Total $286

Positioned to make a statement from the entry, the new table still draws the eye to the window. Glass-top tables are nice options for staging purposes because they're visually light and bounce light around a room.

RIGHT: Repositioning overhead lighting was key to bringing order to the room. This chandelier centered above the table teams with four recessed lights that direct light elsewhere in the room. **OPPOSITE TOP:** For the ultimate in color continuity, Lisa staged the room with flowers that match the new window treatments.

> lessons learned

> DON'T PLAY GUESSING GAMES. Buying a house is serious business, and house hunters are in no mood for games. Take the guesswork out of their tour by making sure every room is instantly recognizable. This room's identity, for example, wasn't clear until it was staged with a large dining table visible upon entering the room. Buyers need to "get it" if you expect to get offers.

> MOVE TO IMPROVE. You've probably created a comfort zone as to how your furnishings are placed, but getting top dollar from a home often requires changing things. To create a better flow, make a room feel larger, or make its purpose more obvious, rearrange the furniture—even remove a few pieces or bring better-suited ones in from another room. Experiment until you find the best placement, and be brave. Positioning an item or two away from walls may seem drastic, but it's often the most effective way to stage a space.

> HAVE A CAN-DO ATTITUDE. Recessed lighting—called "can" lighting—is one of those little touches that makes a home feel brighter and newer. A few can lights installed along the perimeter of a room or in the corners can shed new light on a dark space, and the streamlined look (the rims of the lights are flush with the ceiling) has mass appeal. While you're at it, consider replacing dingy light switches and switch plates for nice, bright white ones. It's a little touch that makes a house seem newer, and therefore more valuable.

> LOOK AT THE HORIZON. When restyling a room, look beyond its four walls. What buyers see through doorways and windows is important. When the space is open, it's even more important to pay attention to what's on the horizon. This dining room opened to the kitchen, so Lisa hung new curtains in the kitchen to create continuity between the two spaces.

KITCHENS and BATHS

When you're measuring the value of a makeover, head to the kitchen or bath—two hardworking areas with selling power. These rooms show how to cash in on style.

> the little kitchen that could

Devoid of style and lacking function, this small kitchen makes
a big comeback—and more importantly gains a place for dining.

BEFORE

WHAT'S WRONG with this room? Just because a kitchen is small, it's no excuse for forgetting about style—at least not for real estate expert Donna Freeman. "This kitchen is so uninteresting," she says. Dated tile countertops clashed with the flooring. A single wooden chair in a corner seemed like a place someone would send a child for time-out, and essentially rendered that part of the room useless. "It's totally wasted space," Donna says. "Let's show them what this space can be used for."

What once was wasted space is now a cozy breakfast nook. The cocktail-height dining set draws attention to the view out the window and is perfect for the small space.

ACTION PLAN Make the room sizzle. A table will be added to an unused corner to improve the room's function, and the countertop will be updated. The room is also overdue for other cosmetic changes. "I really want to make it feel like a kitchen you would invite guests into while you're cooking," interior designer Lisa LaPorta says.

> construction zone

If you have a few small projects that require special skills, be resourceful to prevent labor costs from walloping your wallet. These three tips can be budget-saving tools.

> **GET FREE HELP.** Recruit handy friends and relatives for the day; you'll be pleasantly surprised at the expertise a group of friends can provide. The price you have to pay in treating them to pizza will be far less than you'd pay a contractor. Just make sure you're not tackling too much: Shoddy work is usually worse than leaving things intact.

> **USE THE BARTER SYSTEM.** Swap jobs with your electrician neighbor or handyman friend. Offer to paint their kitchen walls, wash their cars, or babysit in exchange for a few hours of labor.

> **CUT A DEAL.** If you have to hire someone, ask if there are ways to reduce the costs, such as if you handle the cleanup and removal of debris.

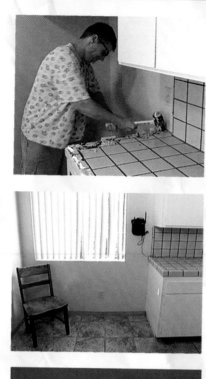

THE MAKEOVER Because buyers would have a difficult time getting past the dated tile countertop, the *Designed to Sell* team decided to do some demolition. The $140 white laminate countertop Lisa chose instantly brightened the space and gave it a modern sensibility. Choosing laminate also removed concerns about keeping grout lines clean. Another smart investment was the $227 Lisa spent on furniture: The dinette set situated near a window established a place to relax while enjoying a meal or cup of coffee. New hardware on the cabinets and new light fixtures were quick fixes that also helped the kitchen sparkle. An earthy-color paint on the walls, tailored valances, and bright accessories brought much-needed style points and coziness to the room. "This is quite a handsome kitchen," Lisa says.

> "I really want to make it feel like a kitchen you would invite guests into while you're cooking."
> —designer Lisa LaPorta

New valances and a warm neutral paint on the walls make the white cabinetry seem almost new. Staging the table and counter with plates helps buyers envision themselves sitting down for a meal.

Creamy-white laminate countertops blend with the setting and complement, rather than compete with, the flooring.

> budget breakdown

Furniture $227

Countertop $140

Lighting $91

Hardware and
accessories $83

Paint and supplies $25

Window treatments $15

Total $581

RIGHT: Flowers—fresh and framed—add a burst of color on the table and walls. For inexpensive artwork, mount photos or pages from a calendar in an old frame refreshed with paint.

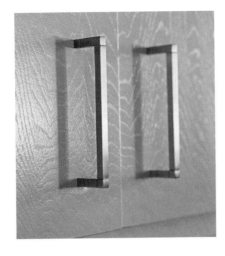

RIGHT: Shiny new hardware updates the cabinets. Adding new hardware provides a quick kitchen facelift. **FAR RIGHT:** This ceiling fixture—one of two installed in the room—is an easy update for less than $50.

CHA-CHING! Most people would jump at the chance to earn an extra $5,000 in 10 days. That's essentially what these homeowners did by rolling up their sleeves with the *Designed to Sell* team and then getting an offer for $5,000 above their asking price the day after the open house. See "Making Sense of Space," page 62, and "From All White To Just Right," page 156, for the other makeovers in the home.

> lessons learned

> **SQUEEZE IN FUNCTION.** Some kitchens are simply too small for a table, but don't give up until you try. Buyers perceive value in an eat-in kitchen. Drop-leaf tables, pub tables, cocktail tables, and bistro tables designed for outdoor use are options for tiny spaces. Reducing the number of chairs—use two instead of four, for example—is another option for size-challenged kitchens.

> **DESIGN FOR THE TIMES.** House hunters know it takes lots of money to remodel a kitchen, which is why they look for one that's already updated. If your kitchen is a blast from the past, find thrifty ways to modernize it. Replacing countertops, as Lisa did here, can totally transform the look. Other affordable updates include covering old flooring with peel-and-stick tiles and painting dark cabinets.

> **SET THE TABLE.** Staging a kitchen table with plates helps buyers envision themselves dining there. The colorful mix of plates and bowls Lisa placed in this kitchen also provide visual appeal. If your plates aren't worthy of display and you don't have the money to buy a few new ones, a vase of fresh flowers placed on the table will suffice to add color.

> **GIVE IT SOME STYLE.** Because kitchens are hardworking spaces, it's easy to neglect them from a style standpoint. Big mistake. Even if a kitchen is small, buyers still want it to look homey. Have fun decorating a kitchen; it's one of the few rooms where everyday items can be put on display. For example, pans can be hung on a rod as artwork on an empty wall, and plates can be stacked on a countertop to add a splash of color.

> living larger

Aside from knocking down walls and spending thousands of dollars, you can't do much about a small kitchen…or can you? A big decluttering and a few light-enhancing touches visually expand this tiny kitchen on a limited budget.

BEFORE

WHAT'S WRONG with this room? Though real estate expert Shannon Freeman realized there wasn't much that could be done about the kitchen's small footprint, she knew the space could live larger than it did. The biggest culprit? Cluttered countertops. "When you have a small space like this, you have to maximize it by showing off the countertops," Shannon says. "If something isn't adding to your value, get rid of it."

Hanging the valance near the ceiling prevents excess fabric from blocking the view and natural light. Low-profile accessories on the window ledge provide interest without impeding the view. New lighting under the cabinets brightens the setting.

ACTION PLAN Create the illusion of space. The cluttered countertops, as well as the knickknacks on the window ledge and elsewhere, need to be cleared. A dated, patterned linoleum floor also was adding a busy look to the room.

ABOVE AND RIGHT: Candles and flowers bring color into the kitchen without locking buyers into a color scheme they may not like.

"When you have a small space like this, you have to maximize it by showing off the countertops. If something isn't adding to your value, get rid of it."

—*real estate expert Shannon Freeman*

THE MAKEOVER Having earmarked nearly all of her $2,000 budget for the combination living room and dining area just off the kitchen, interior designer Lisa LaPorta embarked on a plan of simple abundance. New under-cabinet lighting showcases the tile countertops—that are now void of clutter that had made the kitchen seem jumbled. "The under-cabinet lights really add a lot," she says. "They give the illusion of space, so it was really a worthwhile investment." New vinyl tiles neutralize the patterned flooring. (See "Installing Vinyl Tiles," page 185, for steps on laying self-adhesive flooring.) Fresh paint and a few well-placed accessories that draw the eye out the window also help the space live larger. Though the projects were limited and small in scope—they tallied up to just $163—the results were big. The space seems larger, cleaner, and newer. "This kitchen now looks like a valuable piece of real estate," Lisa says.

> wick tip

Candles are an inexpensive way to accessorize a room and add emotional appeal. To give new candles, and therefore your room, a less-staged look, light the wicks and let them burn a bit. The blackened wicks—and even some melted wax dripping down the sides—create a cozier, lived-in look. Similarly a new taper can be broken to create two or more candles from one, conjuring images of hours of flickering light. For safety reasons candles shouldn't be burned when buyers are going through your home unless you have a trusted adult standing guard.

LEFT: Peel-and-stick vinyl tiles that mimic the look of natural stone give the formerly busy floor a quick and stylish update for just $70.

Good room design factors in the flow to and from other rooms. Tile countertops visually connect the dining area's wet bar to the kitchen. The bar's formerly dark cabinetry clashed with the lighter-tone kitchen cabinets. Neutralized with paint, the bar now blends into its surrounding, allowing the eye to move toward the kitchen window. New neutral-color flooring in both rooms helps make an easy transition between the spaces.

> budget breakdown

Flooring $70

Lighting $65

Paint and supplies $20

Window treatments $8

Total $163

> lessons learned

> **CLEAN SELLS.** It goes without saying that a house that's up for sale should sparkle from floor to ceiling. Clean also is a state of mind. A room overloaded with knickknacks and other items, as this one was, tends to create a mental image of filth—even if surfaces are squeaky clean.

> **EMBRACE YOUR BUDGET.** When you're trying to spruce up your house, money seems to fly out the windows. But as Lisa showed with this $163 makeover, there's no reason to be deterred by a small budget. When money is tight, just be resourceful about how it's spent. Rank your room's weaknesses, and then address the top one or two shortcomings. Paint is always a good investment—and one with payback—because freshly painted walls can make a room sparkle.

> **MAKE COUNTERS PRODUCTIVE.** Kitchen countertops are notorious clutter catchalls. For daily living it may be nice to have the coffeemaker, blender, toaster, and other items at your fingertips, but when you're showing your house they need to find an out-of-the-way home. To create the illusion of space, countertops should be void of just about everything. The items that remain should be for staging purposes to help portray a homey environment. In this kitchen a bouquet of purple flowers and three lavender candles are strategically placed on either side of the sink to draw the eye out the window above it.

> **SEE THE LIGHT.** In small spaces light is key to visually expanding a room. To that end, Lisa had lights installed under the cabinets to give the illusion of more countertop space. She also replaced a lacy window treatment with a simpler valance, hanging it at ceiling height to keep the fabric from blocking too much light.

CHA-CHING! Two weeks after the open house, the homeowners sold their townhouse for $30,000 more than similar ones in the complex. (See "Separate But Equal," page 38, to check out the changes the *Designed to Sell* team made in the combination living/dining room.)

> kitchen resuscitation

Cleanliness may be a virtue in a space designed for cooking, but this kitchen was cold and clinical-looking—plus it didn't function well. A richer paint color and a spiffy new cabinet unit bring the room to life.

BEFORE

WHAT'S WRONG with this room? What's not to love about a kitchen with white walls, white cabinets, a white sink, and white appliances? After all the more neutral a room is the more appealing it is to buyers, right? Not quite, says real estate expert Shannon Freeman. "The kitchen is the heart of a home, and this one isn't even beating," she says. Though clean and pristine, the all-white scheme was cold and lifeless—not exactly a buyer-pleasing aesthetic. A table placed below a series of upper cabinets made an awkward eating space, Shannon also notes.

Accessories and
a stylish window
treatment bring color,
texture, and visual
interest into the
formerly stark white
kitchen. The golden
yellow hue in the
stripes of the fabric
and on some of the
accessories adds
visual warmth.

ACTION PLAN Find a pulse. The stark kitchen needs color and texture to make it warm and inviting. Because the room is small, every item in it needs to have maximum function. The table placed below a series of upper cabinets doesn't. The table needs to go and the space reconfigured so the area under the cabinets is more usable.

RIGHT: The new countertop is a near-perfect match to the existing tile counter, creating a seamless look. Open shelving prevents the small kitchen from seeming closed in. Wicker baskets offer textural contrast to the tile, and cue buyers as to how to keep this storage area from looking cluttered. **OPPOSITE:** Accessories in varied sizes and shapes give the room visual rhythm. Yellow accessories elsewhere in the room help create a cohesive look.

"You can never have too much storage or too much counter space in a kitchen."
—*designer Lisa LaPorta*

THE MAKEOVER To warm up buyers, interior designer Lisa LaPorta knew she would need to take the chill out of the room—and that she could easily do it. "Paint color is key to giving this kitchen a heartbeat," she says. Golden-beige paint veered the room from hygienic hospital lab to cozy cooking space, and allowed the white cabinetry to pop. ("People like white cabinets," Lisa says.) A new French door welcomes natural light. The added boost of sunlight helps the small room sparkle while visually enlarging it by blurring the boundary between the indoors and out. Removing the table that sat underneath a series of upper cabinets near the door opened up space for a counter and shelving unit—a much more functional option for the awkward area. Painted white and topped with white tile, the new unit blends seamlessly with the existing cabinets. "You can never have too much storage or too much counter space in a kitchen," Lisa says.

> working with white

When it comes to cabinetry and appliances, classic white is a favorite. And in many kitchens that are ready to go on the market, white is often the best choice due to its widespread appeal. Consider these tips for seeing the light with white.

> **FIND THE RIGHT WHITE.** If you're planning to paint cabinets or trim, choose a white that works with the room's lighting and surface materials. Not all whites are created equal: Some have undertones of blue, pink, yellow, gray, or brown. Take home paint chips in different tones to see how the white you're considering looks in the room and how natural light changes the look throughout the day.

> **THINK "WHITE PLUS ONE."** This is the easiest color combination there is: Any color goes with white. Be mindful that white will make virtually any color pop—even a pale one— when placed against it. To appeal to the most buyers, team white with another neutral color rather than a bolder color that will only be accentuated due to the contrast.

> **ADD TEXTURE.** Texturally rich items can tone down the harshness of a white setting. Throw rugs or wicker baskets are little accents with potentially big impact.

CHA-CHING! "Kitchens are so important, and this kitchen is in great shape," Lisa says. So great, in fact, that it factored in to the sellers receiving three offers the day of the open house. They sold the house for $16,000 above their asking price. (Check "Small Changes, Big Impact," page 50, to see how the *Designed to Sell* team transformed the living room for just $257.)

> budget breakdown

French door	$281
Accessories	$209
Counter and cabinet	$183
Paint	$30
Total	$703

A new French door has a twofold purpose: It lets natural light into the space and visually expands the room to the outdoors. Installing a Roman shade above the door, rather than covering it with miniblinds or another treatment, gives buyers an unimpeded look at the new feature and maximizes the view. The shade still can be lowered for privacy.

> lessons learned

"FINE" DOESN'T BRING TOP DOLLAR. Like most people you've probably sized up a room, shrugged, and halfheartedly declared "It's fine." While there may not be anything terribly wrong with the room—like this kitchen, it may be clean, functional, and updated—it lacks oomph. That doesn't cut it when you're trying to wow buyers and entice them to ante up. Pinpoint the lackluster rooms in your home, and come up with a plan to take them from fine to fabulous. If the list is too long to tackle in your allotted time frame, focus on the room that will yield the biggest payback. Kitchens and baths always score big with buyers.

BE COUNTERINTUITIVE. Buyers want to be able to envision themselves having elbowroom for prepping foods, preparing meals, and unpacking grocery bags. All of those tasks require ample counter space. If your kitchen is short on counter space, get creative. A small freestanding island adds work space. An over-the-range microwave or a microwave shelf will free up counter space. Even replacing a standard table with a counter-height one gives the impression of additional work space. The best way to gain counter space is also the easiest: Keep the countertops clear (except for a few accessories) to give the illusion of more space.

WARM UP TO NEUTRALS. When real estate agents direct sellers to neutralize their homes, they're not implying that walls should get a fresh coat of play-it-safe white. As this kitchen showed, a too-white room is cold and lifeless. When you think neutrals, step out of the box. A neutral color can be a golden wheat, a khaki, or even a sage.

If you must have white, choose one with warm undertones. A paint dealer can help you see the differences between a stark white and one that has warmer reddish or yellow undertones, for example. But remember, paint tends to look darker after it goes on the walls.

CREATE CONTINUITY. Renovating is tricky when it requires matching new items to existing ones. Before you get too gung ho, make sure you know where to find suitable matches to existing elements so buyers don't question or attention to detail. In this kitchen the new countertop is a close match to the existing one, and the new cabinet was painted white for continuity. If you can't find the materials to match what you have, revise your plan. Shoddy updates invite shoddy offers.

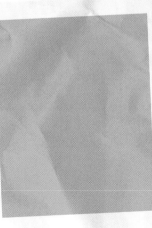

> clean sweep

There's no room for disarray when a house is on the market. This once cluttered and unfocused bath is now a tidy space that takes advantage of its best feature: the view out the window.

BEFORE

WHAT'S WRONG with this room? Real estate expert Donna Freeman isn't one to mince words. "This is a buyer's nightmare," she says of the bathroom that is cluttered with lotions, perfumes, hair dryers, and other grooming items strewn about the vanity and on countertops. "A buyer doesn't want to come in here and really touch anything because these are personal items of the seller's," she says. The room's leaded-glass windows are its saving grace: "With these lovely windows, I'm sure the bathroom really could be quite nice," she says.

Showy leaded-glass windows that span the back wall set the tone for the makeover. A busy green-and-white checked valance was removed to allow a full view outdoors and to usher in as much natural light as possible.

ACTION PLAN Make the room sparkle. Personal items need to be put away. The flooring and shower/tub unit need to be updated, and the leaded-glass windows should shine. With so much clutter, it seems like a huge task. "It's like someone set off an ugly bomb in here," one homeowner admits.

> flooring factors

Forget "anything goes" when it comes to bathroom flooring. The carpeting in this bath, for example, was an odd choice for a moisture-prone space and a sure turnoff to buyers. Bathroom floors should be durable and water-resistant (that means no carpet or wood), but not slippery when wet. Natural stone brings a luxurious look into a bath. Smooth, glossy stones can be slippery; for better traction choose a honed finish. More porous stone, such as limestone, is susceptible to staining and pitting, and must be sealed to prevent damage. To get the most bang for your selling buck, consider vinyl, which is a lower-cost alternative to stone. Vinyl tiles come in a wide selection of styles, including ones that resemble stone.

"By putting neutral colors in this room, the green outdoors pops."
—designer Lisa LaPorta

Interior designer Lisa LaPorta dug into her bag of design tricks to visually enlarge the somewhat small bathroom and create a more serene environment. Green carpeting that was vying for attention with the great view out the windows was replaced with neutral-color vinyl tiles. "By having the green on the floor, you didn't notice the green out the window as much," Lisa says. A checked valance that partially covered the windows was removed and the windows left bare to show off the leaded detailing as well as the view. "By putting neutral colors in this room, the green outdoors pops," Lisa says. Another space-expanding element is the clear doors on the shower/tub unit. A bonus is that the backyard is now visible from the shower. Simple accessories and a major decluttering restore order to the countertops. A bouquet of flowers and glass accessories put a fresh spin on a space that once screamed utilitarian. With the clutter gone and the space neutralized, buyers attending the open house honed in on the leaded-glass windows—which are what Donna and Lisa wanted the focus to be. "It really shows off the amazing backyard," Lisa says. "Because of the simple and neutral design, that is what buyers will look at."

New vinyl tiles that mimic the look of stone are an $85 improvement with dramatic results. The peel-and-stick tiles replace carpeting, which isn't the best option for a bathroom.

RIGHT: Clear shower doors common to high-end baths give this older shower and tub unit a spa-like look which visually expands the room in the process. Tile and grout must sparkle in order to carry off a see-through door.

> **budget breakdown**

Shower doors	$418
Flooring	$85
Accessories	$45
Paint and supplies	$40
Total	$588

CHA-CHING! If you're not convinced of the value of sprucing up and staging your home, consider this: These homeowners received multiple offers and ended up selling their house for $50,000 above what comparable homes in the area were getting. (See "Elegant Upgrade," page 138, and "Perfect Fit," page 32, for the two other room makeovers that contributed to the selling success.)

> lessons learned

> FIND THE EASY MONEY. It's difficult for sellers to get enthused about sinking lots of money into a house they'll soon leave—so don't. Look for low-cost improvements that will reap big rewards. The peel-and-stick vinyl tiles used in this space updated the bathroom's entire look for just $85. Focus on smaller details too. Paint designed for porcelain camouflaged the old tub's imperfections. Metallic spray paint gave the frames of the recessed light fixtures a shiny new disposition. Checked towels, which matched the valance and throw rugs, were replaced with neutral-color ones for spa-inspired serenity. Even something as simple as dusting light bulbs can make a room seem brighter.

> AVOID COMPETITION. New neutral-color tiles ensure that the floor, once covered in green carpeting, no longer commands attention. The splash of color is now left to Mother Nature, which means buyers are drawn to the focal-point windows and the view beyond. To determine if items in your rooms are waging war with one another, mentally note where your eye goes when you enter the room. If you're bouncing back and forth between two elements, decide which one deserves top billing. Removing a strongly patterned throw rug, for example, can easily shift the focus away from a floor.

> PURGE THE PRODUCTS. Bathrooms are personal enough spaces on their own without buyers having to be subjected to a stranger's toothbrushes, razors, and other grooming and hygiene products. Clear off countertops and shower ledges, as well as any behind-the-door hooks where pajamas roost. Drawers and medicine cabinets also should be tidy because buyers will be opening those. Pretend you have a big eraser, and go from room to room to remove personal items, such as notes on the refrigerator, awards hanging on an office wall, and an abundance of family photos on a mantel or shelves.

> EXPECT THE UNEXPECTED. When the *Designed to Sell* team removed the existing shower doors, they damaged some of the ceramic tile. Later water gushed from a pipe that was sliced accidentally. "You never know what you're getting into when you do construction," Lisa says. When you're faced with a setback, stay calm and remain focused on the big picture: more offers and more money. Of course to get that you'll need to repair the damage that's been done.

> luxury despite limitations

A small and dingy bath earns bonus points as a clean and stylish space to help this home exceed its initial selling potential.

BEFORE

WHAT'S WRONG with this room? Not only did this bathroom lack size, it lacked style. Dated elements—including the countertop, tub backsplash, and floor—made the space look dingy. A nondescript light fixture, frameless mirror, and standard-issue towel bars gave the room a cheap, move-in, move-out apartment feel. "Nothing about this bathroom stands out to me," says real estate expert Shannon Freeman.

Staged with flowers, candles, and crisp white towels, the vanity area is a striking focal point. The new mirror reflects the window, which is dressed with a simple valance that softens the look.

"Nothing about this bathroom stands out to me."

—real estate expert
Shannon Freeman

ACTION PLAN Command attention. Modernize and neutralize the room with a new countertop and flooring and by removing the wide backsplash on the tub. Spark a spa-like style through accessories and new hardware.

The flecked pattern of the new countertop mimics the look of stone and provides visual interest.

> getting bucks from the bath

If you're wondering where to put your money to help you get top dollar from your home, a bathroom is a good investment. People may or may not make an offer based on the condition of these much-used spaces. A new countertop can dramatically update the bath, making the cabinetry or other elements seem newer by association. A decorative mirror, rather than a medicine chest or frameless mirror, is another way to give a hardworking space visual interest. The best thing of all, though, is elbow grease. Every surface should sparkle! After the critical cleaning is done, you can add extra touches of warmth and character.

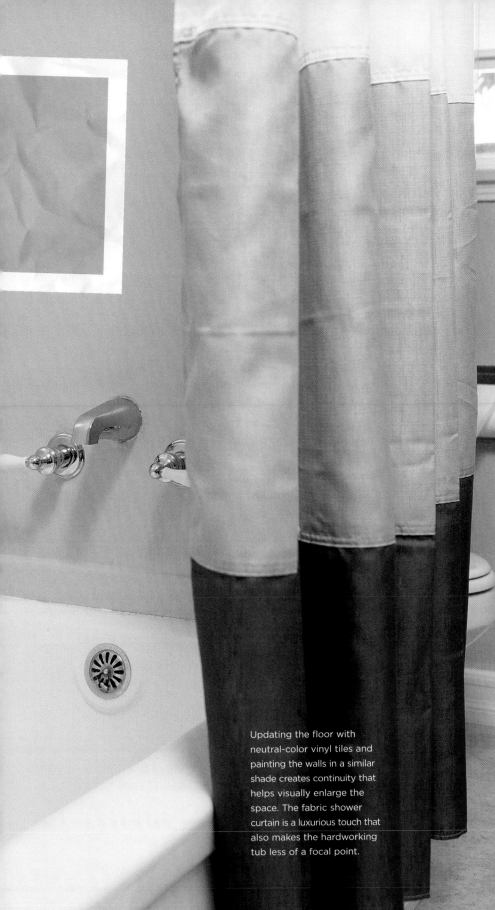

Updating the floor with neutral-color vinyl tiles and painting the walls in a similar shade creates continuity that helps visually enlarge the space. The fabric shower curtain is a luxurious touch that also makes the hardworking tub less of a focal point.

THE MAKEOVER Interior designer Lisa LaPorta knew she couldn't alter the size of the room—at least not structurally—but she could make it seem bigger, brighter, and more luxurious through cosmetic improvements. She focused most of her budget on the vanity area to make it a stunning focal point. A new countertop that mimics the look of stone was a $63 investment that on its own made the room seem newer and fresher. A large framed mirror above the vanity creates a stylish grooming spot, visually enlarging the space and reflecting the paned window—a bonus in what is often a windowless space. The dingy tub also received a facelift, with the wide, dated backsplash removed and the drywall behind it repaired and repainted for a more streamlined look. And the floor enjoyed a big style boost for just $38: Vinyl tiles placed on the diagonal create a showy new surface underfoot. A fabric shower curtain with bands of cream, taupe, and brown fabrics sets the room off on an elegant new journey. Smaller decorative touches, such as replacing a standard-issue towel bar by the vanity with a towel ring that fits the space better, further the spa-like look.

> budget breakdown

Accessories	$344
Hardware and lighting	$73
Countertop	$63
Flooring	$38
Paint and supplies	$21
Lumber and drywall	$20
Total	$559

RIGHT: Removing an ugly, wide laminate backsplash from the tub was a necessity from a style standpoint. The *Designed to Sell* team had to repair drywall that was damaged in the process, but the extra effort was worth it for this more streamlined backsplash.

CHA-CHING! When you're selling a house it's all about creating a buzz, which the *Designed to Sell* team did here. The dramatic changes in the bathroom and the living/dining room (see "Aging Gracefully," page 80) helped the homeowners get 16 offers in just three days. The house sold for $26,000 above the asking price.

> lessons learned

DON'T THROW MONEY DOWN THE DRAIN. A tub or shower that's showing its age—whether from soap scum, style, or color—won't earn you extra money. If replacing a dated unit isn't possible, make it sparkle with new fixtures, new caulking, and a thorough cleaning. Hanging a luxurious fabric shower curtain can camouflage the tub or shower's shortcomings.

SET THE STAGE. Because bathrooms are usually limited in size, every surface and feature count. Create drama with a decorative mirror (skip a nondescript medicine chest), a showy shower curtain, crisp white towels that conjure images of a spa, candles, and flowers. A plush white robe draped over the tub is another subliminal message that this is a room to enjoy.

COUNT ON THE COUNTER. A new countertop works wonders in a bathroom without demanding a big price tag. Inexpensive countertops with recessed sinks are widely available at home centers, offering an in-a-day update. The new countertop installed in this bathroom single-handedly updated the look of the cabinetry and the room as a whole. If needed paint the cabinetry to give it an even fresher look.

CLEAN UP YOUR ACT. No one likes to see reminders of other people's gunk. Soap scum on shower walls, mold or grime in the caulking around a tub or sink, and toothpaste caked to the side of a sink are a few bathroom realities that can make a buyer scramble. Your house isn't ready to show until every surface in the bathroom is clean. Bathrooms are huge on buyer's lists, so make yours worthy.

A bouquet of flowers
brings additional
color and texture
into the room.

> bathing beauty

This ugly duckling bathroom evolved into a swan after its wallpaper and dated fixtures were removed. Though small, the space exudes luxury.

BEFORE

WHAT'S WRONG with this room? Pink wallpaper. Perhaps no two words have less selling power than these, but that's what this space had to offer. "This entire bathroom is stuck in a time warp—from the pink, horrible wallpaper to the gold fixtures to the light box," real estate agent Shannon Freeman says. "I can't imagine that this bathroom is going to appeal to any buyers."

A two-color palette helps the bathroom make a simple but striking statement. The fabric shower curtain—hung from a rod at ceiling height for extra drama—is a luxurious touch.

**ACTION PLAN** Step into the modern world. To give the space mass appeal, the pink wallpaper has to go. The dated light box that was casting shadows over the room is also on the "out" list, as is the hardware on the cabinets. The underlying goal is to give the utilitarian space some style.

> bath splash

Because most bathrooms tend to have a fair amount of white in them (on sinks, tubs, tiles, and so forth), a "white plus one" color scheme is a foolproof option, and one that can help visually expand a less-than-grand space by keeping things simple. Consider pairing white with beige or gray to create a soothing spa-like look with widespread appeal. Though plush white towels may not be practical for daily use, their crisp, clean look is ideal for staging purposes.

ABOVE: Embroidery on the curtain tieback is a small detail that provides a lush look. **RIGHT:** Silvery accents sparkle in the small space. If you don't have the money to buy new knobs or fixtures, give existing ones a thorough cleaning to make them shine.

THE MAKEOVER

The *Designed to Sell* team had an obvious first task in this bath: stripping the wallpaper. Painting the newly cleaned walls in a pleasing taupe was a great improvement on its own, but the improvements didn't stop there. Removing a bulky and dated light soffit paved the way for more natural light to stream in from a skylight. Two chrome light fixtures installed above the mirror that spans the vanity and silvery knobs on the cabinet doors and drawers give the room a modern edge. A fabric shower curtain hung at ceiling height, gracefully swept to the side, and held back with an embroidered tieback mimics a luxurious drapery panel that would dress a window.

Silver-tone light fixtures give the bath a modern update for just $88. If new fixtures aren't an option, metallic spray paint is often a better alternative than leaving dated fixtures as is.

> budget breakdown

Lighting fixtures	$88
Shower curtain	$65
Hardware	$59
Paint and supplies	$35
Accessories	$25
Total	$272

CHA-CHING! It's almost a given that if the pink wallpaper had remained on the walls the homeowners wouldn't have been able to ask for top dollar. But with their updated bath, as well as living room (see "Four-Star Retreat," page 68) and bedroom (see "Playing Up The Positive," page 144), they garnered $23,000 above their original asking price.

> lessons learned

PEEL THE PAPER. If you're thinking about leaving wallpaper on your walls, consider this incentive: "With every inch of wallpaper that comes off, that's a dollar in your pocket," host Clive Pearse says. Indeed you'll be rewarded in the long run if you take the time to remove wallpaper—especially if it's something as taste-specific as the pink wallpaper in this bathroom. See "Removing Wallpaper" on page 183 of the "Do It Yourself" chapter.

ADD SOME STYLE. Regardless of its size and function, a bathroom is still a part of your home—treat it like one. This small space features a big bouquet on the countertop and a shower curtain that seems more like a luxurious drapery panel. Both elements give an illusion of grandeur.

SEE THE LIGHT. Ceiling-mounted light boxes aren't only unattractive, they can cast shadows on a room or shed harsh light. And because lights should be turned on to brighten a space when potential buyers walk through, you may not be putting your room "in the best light." In this bath stylish three-globe fixtures hung above the mirror replaced a bulky and unattractive light box. The new fixtures direct light to the sink area where it's most needed for grooming purposes. "Updating light fixtures is a simple and inexpensive way to give an entire space a brand-new feel," host Clive Pearse says.

>BEDROOMS

Sound the alarm! There's no room for bland bedrooms when buyers are seeking sleeping spaces that pamper. Let the relaxed luxury of these rooms offer blissful inspiration.

> elegant upgrade

Bedrooms are sanctuaries that allow escape from the daily grind. This messy master needed a "buyer beware" sign on the door before the *Designed to Sell* team gave it focus and soothing sophistication.

BEFORE

WHAT'S WRONG with this room? When real estate expert Donna Freeman stepped into this master bedroom, the first thing that caught her attention was the mess, not the room's interesting architecture. Cardboard boxes, clothes, and other items cluttered the space. A desk with a computer pushed what should have been a relaxing space into a work zone. Dated bedding missed out on an easy opportunity to give the room a modern touch. "It's a disaster; it breaks every single rule," Donna says of the space. "A buyer won't be able to see past this. It's not a relaxing bedroom."

This traditional-style sleigh bed is a welcome departure from the bed that previously occupied the space. (Designer Lisa LaPorta called the quirky, built-in bed "one of the strangest things I've seen.") White shelves maximize the function of the recessed area and subtly contrast with the walls to draw the eye to the sleeping space.

Create a serene scene. In addition to clearing the clutter, the desk and computer need to go to ensure that buyers see the room's rest-and-relaxation potential. An odd bed and nightstand ensemble that is built into the wall of the sleeping cove needs to be torn out and replaced with freestanding furniture that will help buyers envision how their own furnishings could fit in the space.

The fabric's stripes help draw the eye to the window behind the bed. The small round pillow is a counterpoint to the room's angular elements.

RIGHT: A new light fixture makes the cushioned nook reading ready. When showing a house, turn on all the lights to make rooms appear brighter and to draw attention to key features—in this case, the nook. The pillows are placed so they're most visible to buyers entering the room.

THE MAKEOVER To transform the busy bedroom into a quietly sophisticated space, interior designer Lisa LaPorta relied on fabric and paint. A pale earthy hue creates a neutral backdrop, but contrasts just enough with the white-painted ceilings to accentuate the angled architecture. Shelves that maximize a recessed area and the trim on a sitting nook also are painted white to draw attention to these features. A stark-white ceiling beam at the entrance of the sleeping cove was painted a deep reddish brown to complement the new furniture—a strategy that draws the eye upward to the interesting architecture. Fabrics in rich browns, golds, and rusts have a classic design, complementing the traditional-style furnishings. A plumping of pillows on the bed and the built-in seating is the final flourish to beckon relaxation. "I love overstuffed pillows because they look really comfy and cozy," Lisa says. "People want to sit with them. Maybe they'll want to buy the environment that has them—do you get where I'm going here?" Though the improvements were nothing out of the ordinary—just paint and new bedding, window treatments, and furniture—the results were transforming. "There's huge drama going on in this bedroom," Lisa says. "It really does look rich and luxurious. This looks like a bedroom that would command top dollar."

"I love overstuffed pillows because they look really comfy and cozy. People want to sit with them. Maybe they'll want to buy the environment that has them—do you get where I'm going here?"

—*designer Lisa LaPorta*

> magic window

House hunters are eager to find a home with abundant windows because they fill a room with light. Strive to make the most—or even more—of your windows with these tips and techniques.

> **TO MAKE A WINDOW APPEAR TALLER,** hang the rod and treatment at ceiling level, rather that on or just above the window trim. Give narrow windows the illusion of width by hanging panels so they hit just at each side of the window, with the bulk of the panels covering wall space. Cafe curtains or blinds can camouflage less-than-stellar views out a window while still letting some light in.

> **IF A ROOM LACKS INTEREST**—say there's no fireplace, crown molding, or showy art piece to draw attention—make a window the focal point. Hang a treatment that forces the eye to gravitate toward the window due to the fabric's color, pattern, or both.

> **IF YOUR WINDOWS HAVE GREAT DETAILS,** such as panes or showy trim, forgo window treatments altogether. Buyers are more smitten by compelling architectural details than they are with a seller's decorating choices.

A space that housed a desk and computer is now bedroom-worthy. Sheers that are casually knotted and flanked by patterned panels draw attention to the view out the window. Accessories on the dresser are sparse and strategically placed to keep the focus on the outdoors.

> budget
breakdown

Window treatments	$207
Fabrics and pillows	$126
Bedding	$100
Paint and supplies	$50
Lighting	$35
Total	$518

CHA-CHING! The changes in this bedroom, the living room (see "Perfect Fit," page 32), and the bathroom (see "Clean Sweep," page 118)—along with an overall decluttering of the house—helped the sellers get $50,000 above what comparable homes in the area were valued at.

RIGHT: Breezy sheers prevent a too-heavy look on the windows. A roller shade addresses any concerns buyers may have about privacy. **FAR RIGHT:** To make the cushioned nook extra inviting, Lisa propped Euro shams against the walls, then layered two smaller square pillows and one round one for interest. For simplicity and continuity, the fabrics are the same ones used for the bedding and window treatments.

> lessons learned

> **DON'T DISTRACT BUYERS.** A room that is cluttered or that serves a dual purpose, as this bedroom did with the desk and computer, causes buyers to lose their concentration. Instead of taking in the room's features and envisioning themselves relaxing in the space, they're left with unwelcome mental images of messiness and a house without enough room. Your job as a seller is to do the work for buyers so they don't have to guess how a room could function for them.

> **APPEAL TO THE MASSES.** This bedroom's floral fabrics and cutesy accessories lacked sophistication and mass appeal. The new bedding, window treatments, and pillows feature a traditional pattern and rich colors that work for men and women. Accessories are a straightforward mix of candles and a few other simple piece—which, again, appeal to men or women.

> **BRING ON THE PILLOWS.** Especially in a bedroom, adding pillows is an easy way to create coziness or add eye-catching color or pattern in a specific area. "When your pillows look too staged, fluff them up, then give them a karate chop so they'll look more natural," Lisa says.

> **KNOW WHEN TO SPLURGE.** These homeowners smartly decided to purchase new furniture. The rich wood pieces set an elegant tone that moves the room from ordinary to upper-scale. It's worth it to invest in pieces that will work in your new home. If a set is too large, just bring in a few key pieces and save the others until after your move. If new furniture is out of the budget but needed to give a room selling strength, consider renting furnishings.

> **GO EASY ON ACCESSORIES.** The shelves that turn one of this room's angled walls into functional space are outfitted with simple and inexpensive accessories, including candles and bookends that create a sort of sculptural piece. Rather than crowd every inch of space, Lisa chose just a select few accessories. This strategy contributes to the bedroom's streamlined look and presents the space as a personal sanctuary designed for rest and relaxation.

> playing up the positive

Smart use of paint and accessories makes this master bedroom ready for relaxation while showcasing its best features.

BEFORE

WHAT'S WRONG with this room? This master bedroom had a lot going for it: ample size, a vaulted ceiling, and a fireplace. Still, real estate expert Shannon Freeman only saw positives turned into negatives. An unattractive wallpaper border and a dated ceiling fan did nothing to accentuate the soaring ceiling. The fireplace was lost against white walls. And sheers covering the windows cast a drab look on what should have been a spacious light-filled retreat. "They're actually taking money out of their bottom line," Shannon says.

New bedding launches the room's classic style. The tonal pattern adds interest without being overpowering, unlike the patterned area rug that was formerly placed near the bed, drawing the eye to the floor.

RIGHT: To make the fireplace stand out as the room's focal point, the *Designed to Sell* team painted the wall a warm golden tone that's slightly darker than the paint on the other walls. The darker accent color draws the eye to a feature not commonly found in a bedroom.

ACTION PLAN Accentuate the positive. The vaulted ceiling and fireplace need to command more attention, as do the windows which also should be dressed to usher in light rather than block it. The room needs to be decluttered and updated for a more modern look.

> wall to wall

When you're getting out the paint rollers to spruce up your walls, think about continuity from room to room. A home that flows with harmonious hues will help buyers flow through easily too. Instead of a piecemeal approach, plan your palette for the whole house so the colors and finishes play off each other. The easiest approach is to use varying shades of the same color. Choose the top two or three hues on a paint strip, vary those colors in rooms and hallways, and then bring in accessories to provide more visual rhythm and splashes of color.

"It has a nice big vaulted ceiling—but this horrible border. It's just too bad."

—real estate expert
Shannon Freeman

BELOW: Cornice boxes give the windows added presence and the room architectural interest. Three pieces of plywood were joined with L brackets to create the cornice frames, which were then wrapped with batting and covered with fabric.

THE MAKEOVER Never underestimate the power of paint and a few well-chosen accessories. The *Designed to Sell* team transformed the bedroom into a serene and stylish getaway that cashes in on the room's best features. The first visual trick was painting the fireplace wall a warm neutral hue that's a bit darker than the paint used on the other walls. The accent wall commands attention, and the light-color marble fireplace surround—once lost against white walls—stands out. Overhead the lackluster ceiling fan was replaced with a graciously curved iron chandelier that engages the eye and accentuates the vaulted ceiling which is no longer visually compromised by a wallpaper border. On the windows flowing side panels and fabric-covered cornices bring drama and richness into the room without hindering natural light. New bedding and a general cleaning up and clearing out (including removal of a desk that detracted from a window) add to the room's relaxing feel.

THIS PHOTO: An oversize chair helps buyers imagine themselves sinking in to read a book. The mirror is strategically positioned to reflect the chandelier. **LEFT:** The stylish chandelier that replaced a dated ceiling fan helps draw attention to the vaulted ceiling.

> budget breakdown

Accessories	$113
Chandelier	$97
Bedding	$72
Window treatments	$63
Cornices	$62
Paint and supplies	$60
Total	$467

CHA-CHING! Just one week after the open house, these sellers accepted an offer for $23,000 above their original asking price. (To see the other rooms in the makeover, turn to "Four-Star Retreat," page 68, and "Bathing Beauty," page 130.)

ABOVE: Sconces add visual interest to the fireplace wall and complement a large scrollwork piece hung in the living room. Breaking apart matched sets is an easy way to stretch your decorating dollars and provide continuity between rooms. **RIGHT:** Layers of pillows add cozy comfort—just what buyers are looking for in a home.

> lessons learned

> **BE YOUR OWN ARCHITECT.** Buyers love details: Crown molding, window mullions, and chair railings are examples of the little extras that can pay off. If your home lacks them, find decorative touches that achieve a similar effect. In this bedroom, the team created architectural interest at the windows with cornice boxes. Old columns and pediments also can bring dimension to rooms that lack character.

> **DEFINE BY PAINT.** For the cost of a gallon (maybe even just a quart), you can zero in on a room's best feature. In this bedroom the fireplace wall was painted a more saturated color than the other walls to make the fireplace stand out. The key to creating an accent wall is to make sure you really have something worth showcasing. Introducing a different color just for the sake of color won't put extra money in your pocketbook, but color that accentuates a great feature will.

> **BRIGHTEN THE BOTTOM LINE.** The surest way to give any room (barring one that's a complete disaster) buyer appeal is to let in the light. A bright room is more emotionally inviting and seems more spacious. Open curtains—or let windows go bare to really capture the light and the view. Weather permitting, a little fresh air never hurts either.

> **CREATE CALM.** What is it about a favorite luxury hotel or spa that appeals to you? More often than not, it's that the place sets a mood, a feel, a tone of tranquillity. The same goes with selling a house. A master bedroom should have a restful, calming quality to it, as this one does. Think quiet colors, plush pillows and cushions, and less, rather than more, furnishings.

> ready for guests

Aspiring to have an inviting sleeping space for overnight visitors is fine, but this bedroom was overly extroverted. With the volume turned down, it's now a tranquil guest getaway.

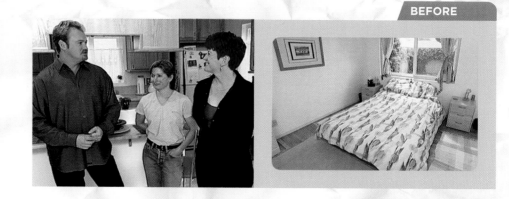

BEFORE

WHAT'S WRONG with this room? This guest bedroom was a breath of fresh air to real estate expert Donna Freeman—but not in a good way. "It's springtime gone very wrong," she says. A bright yellow wall of closet doors and cabinetry was jarring, and a yellow-and-white floral bedspread was dingy and dated. Mismatched curtains and a lackluster ceiling fan made the room's style barometer dip even further. The biggest selling point—a refinished hardwood floor—was barely visible underneath small throw rugs.

The earthy reds and golds of the bedding continue the color scheme that starts with the home's exterior. With the throw rugs removed, the wood floors shine.

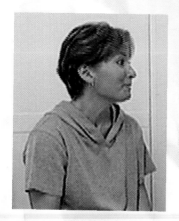

"It's springtime
gone very wrong."

*—real estate expert
Donna Freeman*

ACTION PLAN

Spring into fall. Restyle
the room with an earthy
autumnal palette that has
widespread appeal and
update it with accessories.
Neutralize the yellow
cabinetry and doors with
white paint so buyers
won't be blinded by a
color that has a limited
fan base.

RIGHT: Moving the bed from
below the window to the
adjacent wall gives the room
two focal points and visually
enlarges the space.

THE MAKEOVER Simply rolling white paint over the yellow closet and cabinetry would have been a huge improvement on its own, but the *Designed to Sell* team continued with other easy updates. A neutral paint creates a warm backdrop for new bedding, featuring similar deep red and golden hues found in other parts of the house and on the exterior. (When you're selling a house, it's nice to have a continuous flow of colors.) Drapery panels coordinate with the bedding and wall color, and the throw rugs were tossed out to let the great hardwood floors gleam. A new chandelier helps ensure that the bedroom is a stylish guest getaway from top to bottom.

This simply styled chandelier replaced the ceiling fan. The new fixture was the most expensive update in the room, but still modest at just $127.

> pattern play

When choosing fabrics with patterns, stick with the classics. Stripes and plaids, for example, are gender-neutral choices that have mass appeal. Steer clear of floral prints, especially in a bedroom where they can make the space seem overly feminine. If you must have florals, consider a paisley. Remember that appealing to the masses also means appealing to both sexes.

CHA-CHING! There was no waiting around for the seasons to change for these homeowners: Seven days after their open house, they sold their house for $26,000 above their asking price. Check "Open to Change," page 74, and "Dining by Design," page 92, to see how the *Designed to Sell* team transformed two other rooms in this home.

> budget breakdown

Lighting	$127
Bedding	$72
Paint and supplies	$44
Window treatments	$34
Total	$277

LEFT: This nightstand features three things that should be on a home seller's staging list: candles, a bouquet of flowers, and updated lighting. **RIGHT:** A vibrantly patterned pillow commands attention in a sea of solid-color pillows.

> lessons learned

> **PAINT TO PLEASE.** As much as you may love bold color, showing restraint will put cash in your pocket when you sell your house. We repeat: Warm neutral colors appeal to more home buyers, and your goal is to give your house mass appeal.

> **SHOW THE REAL VALUE.** There's no logic to spending thousands of dollars or precious time and sweat restoring hardwood floors, only to cover them with throw rugs as these homeowners did. Buyers need to be able to see the value if you expect them to make a great offer. Tout your home's selling points by moving the sofa that's blocking a bay window or by pulling back the curtain hiding a beautifully tiled shower.

> **SMALL CHANGES HAVE PAYBACK.** Dramatic results don't require sweeping changes or a big price tag. This bedroom's simple and inexpensive changes involved merely painting and adding a few new accessories. Rearranging furniture was free. The result is a quietly elegant space—one that whispers but still wows.

> **LAYER IN SOFTNESS.** When staging a bedroom, think about layers. At a minimum plump the bed with pillows, as Lisa did in this room. Another soft touch is to drape the foot of the bed with a chenille throw (just toss it on, letting it fall naturally). Adding a downy feather mattress also can make a bed—and room—seem dreamier.

> from all white to just right

This bedroom was a blank slate until the *Designed to Sell* team gave it classic appeal with warm colors and elegant fabrics.

BEFORE

WHAT'S WRONG with this room? With white walls, white bedding, and white window blinds, this master bedroom took depersonalization to the extreme—a little too far to the extreme for real estate expert Donna Freeman. Even the tops of two dressers were bare, sans for a white pitcher on one. "We need something brought in to personalize the room," Donna says. Overhead the white acoustic ceiling—with a bumpy texture commonly called "cottage cheese"—contributed to the lifeless look. "Part of the reason this home feels cold is the cottage cheese," she says. "It belongs in the refrigerator, not in here."

Window treatments frame the view out the sliding glass door and showcase the bonus feature—the balcony. Removing the "cottage cheese" texture on the ceiling updates the space and visually heightens the ceiling.

ACTION PLAN Warm it up. Bring in color through paint and fabrics. The "cottage cheese" texture on the ceiling needs to be removed to update and streamline the room's look, as do the lackluster vertical blinds on the sliding glass door. Framing the glass with curtain panels will put the focus on the outdoors.

LEFT: The stripes and florals of the window treatment fabrics repeat in the bedding for a cohesive look. Purchased bedding ensembles are a near-effortless way to decorate a bedroom, and are great for home sellers pressed for time and in need of a quick cosmetic fix.

> a bumpy ride

Do your ceilings suffer from cellulite? Texture-sprayed ceilings—not-so-lovingly called "cottage cheese" or "popcorn" ceilings—can rough up a sale. Be prepared for buyers who turn their heads up and be proactive about your ceilings. Cobwebs and dirt can get trapped in the bumps, so make sure you've dusted (or even vacuumed) overhead before you show your house. Dingy ceilings require painting. Spraying is usually the best option because a roller can pull off the texture and leave bare spots. If you use a roller, choose one made for rough surfaces, be gentle, and place a drop cloth underneath your work area to catch the "popcorn" that falls off. Time permitting, remove the cottage cheese texture. It's a simple procedure, but a messy one. Attempt it only if your schedule is clear and you can budget for the worst-case scenario of calling in a professional to finish the job or repair the existing surface.

LEFT: The warm tone of the freshly painted walls complements the golden tones of the new bedding.

THE MAKEOVER

The *Designed to Sell* team started at the top by addressing the textured ceiling. The messy job required spraying the ceiling with water (after protecting the floor and walls with plastic), letting it soak in, and then scraping off the mushy plaster to reveal the smooth surface underneath. "Taking the 'cottage cheese' off makes the ceiling feel like it's 2 feet higher," interior designer Lisa LaPorta says. A warm paint color on the walls creates an inviting backdrop for furnishings and accessories, including bedding in rich colors and classic patterns. Dressing the sliding glass door with a matching window treatment draws attention to the balcony—a bonus getaway for buyers. Nightstands with new table lamps flank the bed to finish off this classically inclined retreat.

"Taking the 'cottage cheese' off makes the ceiling feel like it's 2 feet higher."
—designer Lisa LaPorta

CHA-CHING! There were no sleepless nights for these home sellers. One day after the open house, they accepted an offer for $5,000 above their asking price. See "Making Sense of Space," page 62, and "The Little Kitchen That Could," page 100, to view the other makeovers in the home.

> budget breakdown

Window treatments	$119
Bedding	$108
Lighting	$64
Paint and supplies	$40
Total	$331

OPPOSITE: Shapely table lamps bring color and interest into the room. They also provide extra illumination for staging it.
RIGHT: A grouping of pillows gives the bed snuggle-in appeal. Adding pillows is one of the easiest ways to make a room feel cozy and inviting.

> lessons learned

> FOCUS THE VALUE. When you've lived in a home for some time it's easy to take things for granted. This bedroom, for example, had lost sight of its best feature: the balcony and view out the sliding glass door. With colorful new window treatments framing the glass, the room's visual focus is where it should be. Think back on things that first attracted you to the house, and make sure to give them prime billing.

> DEPERSONALIZE, NOT DEPRIVE. There's a fine line between depersonalizing a room and making it seem lifeless. This bedroom had crossed the border to the latter. When ridding your rooms of personal items, do it in stages. Remove a few items, step back, and then remove a few more items if needed. One or two pictures on a dresser is fine; five or six is a crowd. Rooms need to look livable, just not lived-in.

> COMPLETE THE PICTURE. There are certain bedroom essentials: a bed, dresser, bedside table, and lamp. Buyers will be trying to figure out how they'd get those essentials in the room, so show them yourself. With nightstands now flanking the bed and table lamps in strategic places, this room answers the call for convenience. Similarly a coordinated bedding and window treatment ensemble gives the room a finished look. The goal? A room where buyers can picture themselves.

> LOOK UP. Don't be so focused on the things at eye level that you forget to give ceilings the once-over. Ceilings—the "fifth wall" of a room—need attention too. The "cottage cheese" texture on this bedroom's ceiling dated the room. Cobwebs can give house hunters the impression of a poorly maintained house. Cracks or peeling paint are more serious red flags, and need to be repaired before showing your house.

>SPECIAL SPACES

Put the often-neglected areas of a home on your to-do list so you can pound out the profits. Take some tips from this revamped courtyard and garage to get motivated.

> seeing clearly

This home's curb appeal was a bit confused, with a nondescript gated entry that led to a difficult-to-identify front door. With more distinguished doors and spruced-up landscaping, the home presents a unified front and gives a good first impression.

BEFORE

WHAT'S WRONG with this yard? It's never a good sign when someone approaches a home and has to ask, "Where's the front door?" That was the question of the day when real estate expert Shannon Freeman assessed this home. With the main entry hidden behind a walled and gated courtyard, the only way to access the house seemed to be via a garage door—and a garage isn't exactly the showy entry point Shannon envisioned. She was equally put off by stone pavers that weren't embedded in the landscaping (thereby creating an ankle-twisting safety hazard), and a long, curved asphalt driveway that had seen better days. "It seems a little shabby, so it makes me think 'If the driveway is shabby and not in great shape, what is the rest of the house like?'" Shannon says. "Curb appeal is so important."

Lattice attached to the top of the
courtyard wall adds height without
making the structure seem like a fortress.
New decorative finials on the lattice's
supportive posts offer a custom touch
and a more refined look.

THIS PHOTO: Wooden doors, potted flowers, and a bench create a welcoming front entrance. The glass doors that were in place before the makeover seemed like sliders to a back yard, creating confusion on where the front entrance was. **OPPOSITE:** A new light fixture and metal house numbers—two easy and inexpensive ways to improve curb appeal—reinforce the fact that this is the entrance to the property.

 **ACTION PLAN** For interior designer Lisa LaPorta, the biggest task was solving a seemingly rudimentary issue: How do you get into the house? "The house is missing a very important part of its anatomy, and that would be a clear and defined entryway," she says, concurring with Shannon's assessment. This home was rare in that it essentially had two front entrances: first at the courtyard, and then at the house. In addition to giving the each entrance distinction with new doors, the fencing, landscaping, and driveway need to be revitalized.

THE MAKEOVER With the homeowners agreeing to cover the cost of resurfacing the driveway—a project they started some time ago—Lisa was able to focus on the myriad other projects that needed to be completed in order to entice potential buyers to get out of their cars. New doors were key to creating a more sensible approach: A tall door replaced a short, nondescript gate on the courtyard entrance, and two solid doors replaced the awkward-looking glass doors that served as the front entrance to the house. The new doors are substantial and prominent—and outfitted with shiny new hardware—so as to leave no doubt where visitors should enter. To soften the courtyard's cinder block wall, the *Designed to Sell* team added a band of lattice to the top, and then splurged on mature plantings that add visual appeal and a punch of color. Smaller decorative touches include a new light and house numbers on the post by the courtyard door and pots of colorful flowers placed by the new doors to the house. "This house has a clear and defined entryway now," Lisa says.

> got curb appeal?

When was the last time you took a good look at your house—a really good look? If it's been awhile, it's time to kick the curb appeal into high gear with these strategies:

> **STAND BACK.** Stand at the street or on the property directly across from you to size up your home's curb appeal. Where do your eyes go? They should immediately be drawn to the front door. Jot down elements that are impeding that view. It may be unruly tree limbs, an attached garage, or a picket fence with peeling paint. Often painting the front door a bolder color is the first corrective measure.

> **TAKE A WALK.** Approach your house as a buyer or guest would. Is the journey from car to front door a pretty one or is it one filled with weeds and barren patches? If it's the latter, get out the trimmer and consider creating small flower beds or lining the area with a few potted plants. New hardware on the front door should be at the end of the destination.

> **GET THE RHYTHM.** A lush green lawn is great, but every property also should have a nice sequence as a person moves through it. Landscaped berms, arbors, ornamental trees, and well-groomed hedges provide visual interest and help break up the monotony of a lawn.

RIGHT: To give the courtyard entry the prominence of a home's front door, the *Designed to Sell* team removed the rather flimsy gate, built a door frame that rises above the lattice, and installed a door that shares the same clean lines as the new doors on the house. Painted a muted green, the door blends with the surroundings yet is substantial enough to ensure that a garage door to the right (not shown) is no longer mistaken as the main entry. The mailbox received a coat of metallic spray paint for a quick update.

> budget breakdown

Gate and hardware $417

Front doors $396

Lattice and supplies $202

Plants $170

Lights and accessories ...$101

Total $1,286

> lessons learned

ENERGIZE THE EXTERIOR. Often homeowners are so focused on the inside of their homes that they neglect the outside—a big mistake because the exterior is the first thing buyers see. As Shannon pointed out with this home, flaws on the outside only cause buyers to wonder what's wrong with the inside, and ultimately lead them to drive right by to the next house for sale. Sprucing up the curb appeal will snag buyers from the start.

DESIGN AN ATTRACTIVE ENTRY. Whether your home has one main entry (as most do) or multiple entrances due to a gates or courtyards, attention to detail is important. New hardware—handles, knockers, kickplates—and a grouping of potted plants are easy spruce-ups that every home seller

should do. In this case, these little additions offered beauty and helped define the formerly murky entrance points. The team also found a quick fix for a drab mailbox in a can of metallic spray paint. A new mailbox in brass would cost about $100, but for just a few dollars, the old one shines.

PATIENCE DOESN'T ALWAYS PAY. Mature plantings give the home a welcoming sense of place, not to mention that they just fill in the harsh courtyard wall better than seedlings would have. Small plants and seedlings are fine when you first move into a house. But when you're getting ready to sell, fuller, larger plants may be in order. There's no reason to spend a fortune: Just a few large plants incorporated into the existing landscaping can work

wonders, filling in bare spots or bringing eye-catching color or texture to areas that need it most.

THINK SAFETY. A yard can be an accident waiting to happen. The stone pavers in front of this home's courtyard gate, for example, created a safety hazard because they weren't level with the ground—and one of the sellers admitted to having stumbled on them a few times. Take a safety-minded tour of your property to assess potential risks: nails protruding from a deck, loose porch railing, steps that have settled too far into the ground, gutter extensions that protrude into a walkway. Even if you aren't selling your house soon, there's no reason to get tripped up on what are usually easy and inexpensive fixes.

> regaining a garage

What have you done for your garage lately? If the answer is not much, it's time to focus on this often-neglected selling point. As these homeowners discovered, a tidy garage can jump-start a stalled sale.

BEFORE

WHAT'S WRONG with this room? Sometimes it's best not to know what lurks behind closed doors. Such was the case with this attached garage. What normally would be a sought-after feature was a mess. "This is a junkyard with a door on it," real estate expert Shannon Freeman says. Ironically the cluttered garage also functioned as the home's laundry area—a space that typically exudes cleanliness. "The function of a garage is to, yes, store your cars and, yes, for storage," Shannon notes, "but in this particular case these sellers are in a quandary because the washer and dryer are out here."

Once a dumping ground, this garage is now an impressive picture of tidiness. The freestanding shelves can make the move with the sellers. The freshly painted walls and floor add a crisp, clean look.

With the garage multitasking as the laundry room, space in front of the washer and dryer was at a premium. A ball hung from string suspended from a ceiling beam acts as a red light so drivers know where to stop, thereby allowing access to the machines.

> "An organized and maintained garage gives the impression that all of the details in the house were cared for."
>
> —designer Lisa LaPorta

ACTION PLAN Create a clutter-free zone. An antique car that merely served as a dumping ground for clutter is among the many things in the garage that must go. The space also needs some type of system to keep things organized—or at least to give house hunters the impression of tidiness.

THE MAKEOVER Interior designer Lisa LaPorta knew that getting this garage shipshape wasn't a glamorous task, but it was an important one. "An organized and maintained garage gives the impression that all of the details in the house were cared for," she says. First the obvious: The homeowners cleared clutter, pitching some items and finding a temporary new home for others. After the garage was emptied, the *Designed to Sell* team went to work demolishing rather clunky built-in shelves and hanging new drywall to replace the rotten surfaces. Paint camouflages a less-than-stellar concrete floor; vinyl chips added to the wet paint provide a rich textural look that is steps above a basic painted slab. A row of freestanding shelves creates a tidy look and is a visually lighter alternative to the old built-in shelving. "By staging it with shelves and bins, it really shows off that this garage can be organized and functional, and it really is a good asset to a house," Lisa says.

Designers know that little details make a big difference—even on something as mundane as a garage floor. To give the floor some "wow" factor, the *Designed to Sell* team rolled on epoxy concrete paint, then added "magic sprinkles." Vinyl chips randomly sprinkled on top of the wet paint add a rich look.

> revival tips

Move over closets: Garages are riding a tide of popularity when it comes to organizational systems. Take some cues from custom-designed systems to make your garage look like a million bucks without a big splurge.

> **THINK VERTICAL.** Use walls to expand storage space. Wall-mounted hooks, racks, shelves, and cabinets can give bicycles, ladders, and other items a lift, thereby adding the illusion of more floor space.

> **FRESHEN UP.** Painting the walls and floor is an easy improvement with a big bonus: It forces you to get stuff out and sorted.

> **GET IN THE ZONE.** For the ultimate in organization, group similar items into "zones." Store sporting goods in a "recreational zone," lawn care equipment in a "yard work zone," and holiday decorations in a "seasonal zone." The zone method improves efficiency and offers a quick inventory of what you have to move.

> **THINK SAFETY.** If your garage has an automatic door, make sure the safety reverse mechanism works. Open the door, place a roll of paper towels sideways directly in the path of the door, and then close the door. When the door reaches the paper towel roll, it should reverse into the open position. If the door crushes the roll, it needs to be adjusted.

Look up! Often the answer to gaining storage space in a garage is overhead. Bicycles hung from hooks mounted to the ceiling beams open floor space below, thereby adding valuable square footage. The space above a garage door also can be used for storage, especially for out-of-season items.

> budget breakdown

Drywall, paint, and supplies	$280
Shelves/storage bins	$221
Flooring materials	$123
Total	$624

CHA-CHING! These sellers knew when to hold 'em: Instead of accepting the first offer after the open house, they held out for better ones. Within three weeks they had an offer for $5,000 above their asking price. (See "Side By Side," page 56, to view the revamped living/dining room that also contributed to the homeowners' selling success.)

> lessons learned

> **SHOW SOME TLC.** Garages, basements, attics—who cares? Buyers do! An organized garage, for example, has been proven to speed a house sale and contribute to a higher selling price. These spaces may be able to take some abuse when you're living in a home, but not when you're selling it. Treat them as bonus rooms and valuable square footage. Repair and paint walls, clean floors, and even add a few homey touches such as a nonslip rug at a door entrance.

> **PRESENTATION COUNTS.** Odd as it may seem, even a garage needs to be staged. After all it's still part of your home. The same rules apply to this hardworking space as they do to the main rooms of the house. You want to give the illusion of space (that means move the vehicles out at open house time) and create a tidy atmosphere (house hunters will view a spiffy garage as an indication of the care given to other parts of the home). If the home doesn't have a mudroom, create one in an attached garage by installing a coat rack on a wall by the door and adding some cubbies for shoes. Similarly provide a warm and inviting entry point to the home, just like you would at the front door (think welcome mat, a fresh coat of paint on the door, and new hardware). The entry from a garage should be an idyllic space as opposed to one that shows the drudgery of being a homeowner.

> **THROW, DON'T STOW.** Most everyone is guilty of stashing something in a garage or basement thinking they might need it again some day. Usually that day never arrives, and in the process the space becomes a crowded, cramped black hole. Simplify your life and help buyers see the full capacity of your home by learning how to part with the old. Set an expiration date: If you haven't used something in the past year, get rid of it. Find a good home (a charity, a friend, a family member) for things that are too good to discard.

> **INSPIRE ORGANIZATION.** Not all potential home buyers have vision, so help guide them as to how a room can function. In this garage, plastic storage bins stowed on the freestanding shelves give buyers a mental image of how they could store items. It doesn't matter if the bins are empty or you take the shelves with you when you leave: Organization helps sell a home.

> DO IT YOURSELF

Roll up your sleeves—it's time to restyle your home! Focus on the four areas that follow to give your rooms a big style boost and your yard some curb appeal.

Getting top dollar from a home starts outside. The "package" you present—the paint job on the house, the lawn, the landscaping, the front door—motivates buyers to either stop in or drive on by. Make a good first impression by improving your home's curb appeal. "If it's already great, make it better by adding drama; if it's awful make it good," says interior designer Lisa LaPorta.

To assess your home's curb appeal, act like a buyer. Drive by your house from both directions—*slooowly.* Peeling paint, overgrown bushes, or junk piled by the side of the house will jump out at you when you peruse your property from a distance. Clean up your act. "The last thing you want home buyers to see anywhere around the front or sides of your house is garbage," Lisa says.

On your drive-through, check other homes in the neighborhood to glean ideas on what looks good and what doesn't. Then take a walking tour, first on the sidewalk and then next to the house to examine windowsills, gutters, and other elements that may need attention. "Maintenance, repairs, and cleanup come first," Lisa says. "Once that's done, it's about making it inviting, charming, better than the house next door."

THE HOUSE ITSELF

The condition and even the color scheme of your house gives buyers a clue as to what to expect on the inside. Make sure the structure is in top shape; even changing the color of the shutters or the front door can give a house a boost.

If a whole-house paint job is in order, select three colors: the main color, a complementary trim color, and an accent color for doors and shutters. Choose colors suitable to your neighborhood. Though you don't want to have just another tan house on a street of tan houses, you don't want your house to stick out like a sore thumb. Existing elements, such as the roof color and any brick, need to play into your color decision. If your roof is terra-cotta tile, for example, select a paint color to complement that.

Don't rush into the painting. Select a day that's calm (so the wind won't blow dirt and leaves onto your fresh paint), mild (50 to 90 degrees), and dry (humidity causes cracks). The house's surface temperature must be within the temperature range on the paint can label for proper curing. Paint the west and south sides of the house in the morning to keep you cooler and allow the paint to cure more slowly (direct sunlight can cause blistering and peeling). Move on to the east and north sides in the afternoon. In dry, windy climates, dampen stucco surfaces with water from a garden hose before painting to prevent the paint from curing too quickly.

If you don't have time to paint the entire house, grab a quart and focus on the front door. The door can and should be an attention-getting focal point, and it offers a bit of leeway to experiment—just don't try anything too wild. Lisa's favorite door colors are green, black, red, and white. Choose a shade that complements the style of the house. A traditional house, for example, may be more suited to a deep reddish-burgundy rather than a bright tomato red.

THE FRONT ENTRANCE

If you think your home's front entrance is merely an unnoticed passageway that's gone in a blink, think again. Real estate agents know all too well that awkward moment when they're fumbling to open a

Continued on page 180

> dividing flowers & plants

Stretch your money and fill in barren spots by multiplying perennials.

YOU WILL NEED

- > Established perennials, such as daylilies, coreopsis, hostas, or peonies
- > Spade or garden fork
- > Small sharp tool such as a trowel, garden fork, or hunting knife
- > Compost (optional)
- > Mulch

1 **Determine which plants are suitable for dividing and transplanting.** (Check with friends and relatives too; most gardeners are eager to find a good home for their plants that need to be thinned.) Prolific growers, such as daylilies, don't perform well when they get too thick and must be divided. Others, such as hostas and peonies, ordinarily don't require division but may be divided as a cost-effective way to fill in bare spots. Generally plants should be divided in early spring or fall; consult a nursery for guidelines on your climate.

2 **To divide,** use a spade or garden fork to separate the plant's crown or clump into portions. For clump- or mat-forming perennials, such as ornamental grasses and hostas, slice off segments with a spade without removing the entire plant from the ground. Many perennials, however, don't grow in a manner that lends itself to this. In those cases dig up the entire plant, shake the soil from the roots, and carefully cut or pull apart sections that include both roots and shoots.

3 **Replant the sections as soon as possible.** Dig a hole twice as wide as the clump you're planting. If desired, mix compost into the soil. Plant the division so the buds sit at or slightly above the soil line. If shoots are present, do not bury them.

4 **Water the divisions well.** Add mulch around the plant to retain moisture and protect it from cold temperatures.

TIP: If the plant seems too small to be easily separated into two healthy plants, hold off. Dividing a small plant can harm or kill it.

> flower power

Keep flowers blooming and looking good by remembering to "deadhead," a practice of removing spent blooms as soon as possible after they fade. Deadheading gives plants more energy to rebloom and creates a cleaner appearance. You can pinch or cut off the dead blooms. Both inground flowers and those in containers need to be deadheaded.

Continued from page 178

lockbox on a door. What do the prospective buyers do while they're waiting? They check out the front door and everything around it. Any peeling paint, tarnished hardware, or cracked cement they observe immediately takes money off their offer, say real estate experts Donna and Shannon Freeman.

Whether your home is blessed with a breezy wraparound porch or cursed with a tiny cement stoop, make it stand out and make it welcoming. Lisa's musts include pots of blooming flowers (or a dried wreath, depending on the season), shiny hardware (including the house numbers, kickplate, and light fixtures), and a new doormat. The door itself and the threshold people step over should be in tip-top shape too. "Giving them a package is critical," Lisa says.

Flowers are the easiest staging strategy. When placed in containers, they offer flexibility so you can add pops of color where buyers will notice them most. Groups of pots create a more effective display than a single container. Cluster a trio of pots in the corner of the stoop or in front of a lackluster wall. Stage pots at various levels on steps and small tables, and pair them with hanging baskets for layered interest. For continuity match plants and containers to the style of the house. For example, display foxgloves—a cottage icon—in vintage crates. Nonflowering plants add drama too. A big fern hanging from a shepherd's hook or placed on a small table can fill dull expanses with color and texture.

TREES AND SHRUBS

Don't make your house a secret by allowing trees and shrubs to rule the roost. "A buyer needs to see the house if they're going to be making an investment in it," Donna says.

A tree that hasn't been pruned in years may be an intimidating sight, so start with the obvious. Remove branches that are dead, broken, or rub against other branches. Cut off branches that hang low and interfere with access under the tree, and remove any sucker growth. Although you want instant gratification as a seller, be mindful of the "one-fourth rule": If you've removed one-fourth of the branches, it's best to give the tree a rest for a year before pruning more.

Making proper cuts is good for the health of the tree and creates a tidy look that buyers will appreciate. Try cutting small branches with short- or long-handle shears. If you struggle, switch to a saw. Don't leave unsightly stubs, but don't cut flush with the trunk either. Cut just outside the branch collar—the swollen area where the branch meets the trunk.

Shrubs are a bit trickier. You don't want to butcher them or shear them into unnatural-looking geometric shapes. Restrict the latter for hedges, borders, and topiaries. Control the size and shape of other shrubs by selectively cutting individual shoots back with hand shears. The bloom time of flowering shrubs determines when to trim them. In general prune spring bloomers immediately after they flower. Summer bloomers can be trimmed whenever they're dormant.

THE YARD

Improving your home's curb appeal doesn't require back-straining digging of new beds (though that certainly can help). There are other less labor-intensive ways to glam up your yard. As Lisa suggests with the exterior as a whole, focus on areas that need repairs. Brown or bare spots in the lawn, plastic edging that has popped up from the ground in landscaped beds, or windowsills with peeling paint give buyers a mental image of a poorly maintained home. Sod will give you instant gratification for filling bare patches; remember that new sod needs TLC and daily watering.

From a cosmetic standpoint, there are several quick fixes that have big impact. Mulch is one of them. Like freshly painted walls, landscaped beds with a layer of rich, dark mulch seem newer by association. Mulch also provides weed control and moisture retention. Shredded bark, such as cypress and cedar, is a good option, plus it's inexpensive and easy to find. Planting a flat or two of annuals is another inexpensive investment that adds instant color and cheer. If you'll be showing your house between summer and fall, choose flowers with earthy tones that easily transition between the seasons, such as golden yellow marigolds that blend well with mums, a fall favorite.

Stepping stones also can add charm to landscaped areas; make sure they're embedded into the ground or mulch to avoid creating a tripping hazard. Another decorative touch is landscaping lights, which add style during the day and function at night. Less is usually more with these; solar-powered ones are easiest to install.

A well-tended lawn goes without saying. Mow grass the day before or the day of the open house. Sharp mower blades give the best results. Dull blades make ragged cuts, which brown and give the yard a washed-out look. Blades should be sharpened at least once a season, and preferably three or four times.

> staining a deck

Bring unparalleled polish to a drab deck.

YOU WILL NEED

- > Garden hose
- > Power washer
- > Scrub brushes and rags
- > Semitransparent oil-base stain with UV blockers
- > Paint tray
- > Roller
- > Paintbrush

1 **Check to make sure the deck is suitable for staining.** Some artificial building materials do not accept stain; check with the manufacturer. If your deck is new and made of pressure-treated pine, cedar, or redwood, it should not be stained for at least a year so the wood can dry out. If your deck is new and made of wood composite, wait eight to 12 weeks for it to weather before staining it.

2 **Wash the deck thoroughly** to remove dirt, grit, and any existing finish. (Most decks are big enough to justify renting or borrowing a power washer to make the job go quickly.) Scrub the wood well, rinse thoroughly, and let dry for at least 24 hours (allow extra time if it's humid).

3 **Pour the oil-base stain into the paint tray.** Use a long-handled roller to apply the stain to the deck floor. Use the paintbrush to stain railings and to touch up missed spots. Let dry thoroughly.

4 **If the color isn't as deep as you prefer,** apply a second coat of stain, following the manufacturer's instructions for drying time.

TIP: A stained deck requires upkeep, so if you plan to stay put for several years make sure you're up to the task of restaining. If not leave the silvery-gray patina that untreated hardwood decks attain over the years as is.

> deck check

Make your deck buyer-ready by driving down popped nails with a nail set (for a long-term solution, replace them with galvanized deck screws) and repairing cracked, rotted, or warping boards, steps, or railings. If you don't plan to stain the deck, give it a thorough cleaning with a deck wash and apply a waterproofing sealer to prevent damage.

> walls

Does your home suffer from pink bathroom syndrome? Do you love the chartreuse walls in your living room? How about that veggie wallpaper in the kitchen? Curse the thought! "Wallpaper and other dramatic statements of taste are like tattoos," says interior designer Lisa LaPorta. "And I don't think anyone wants their tattoos chosen by somebody else."

Indeed they don't, which is why the *Designed to Sell* team preaches neutral, neutral, neutral. "If you're staying within a neutral range, it's a good investment," Lisa says. "I would err on the side of boring before I would go outrageous." Paint is cheap, and a little bit of elbow grease can correct brush-and-roller blunders or wallpapering fiascoes (see "Removing Wallpaper," opposite).

PICKING PAINT

To make rooms seem warm and inviting, Lisa recommends using warm neutral paint colors. Her favorite hues include Ralph Lauren's Tangier Island (NA05), Devonshire (NA22), Parchment (NA49), Fairy Wren (NA61), Cotswold Breeches (NA16), and Cymric Silver (TH09). Don't go overboard on a good thing, though. For variety paint hallways in a lighter shade of the color you've selected for key rooms or use a linen—a softer alternative to stark white.

After you've selected the color, you'll need to make a few other decisions. First off: oil or latex? Latex paint has largely replaced oil-base paint for do-it-yourselfers. It dries faster and cleans up with just soap and water. Another decision is the sheen. Flat paint has no shine; gloss has the most shine. The sheen can downplay negatives or accentuate positives. A flat sheen helps hide imperfections. A semigloss or gloss paint can draw attention to details, such as crown molding. A low-sheen paint is usually a good option for walls, and a higher-sheen paint can provide contrast for trim. A quality brush and roller are other wise investments.

PREP TIME

It's tempting to skip the prep work, but remember every crack in the wall or drip on the woodwork means fewer dollars in your pocket. So scrape off loose paint, patch holes and cracks, and sand rough or glossy surfaces to ensure proper adhesion. Wash the walls with water and mild detergent; rinse.

After the surface is clean and dry, use low-tack painter's tape to mask areas you don't want painted. Regular masking tape can pull off paint when removed. Seal the edge of the tape by running your finger over it; a crisp seal prevents paint from seeping through. Lay drop cloths to protect floors and furniture.

THE TECHNIQUE

When painting a wall, start by "cutting in." Use a 2-inch trim brush to apply a 3-inch-wide strip where the wall meets the ceiling, baseboards, windows, and doors. Fill in the remaining areas,

working in 6x6-foot blocks. If brushing apply paint with horizontal strokes first, then vertical strokes over the same area. If rolling apply the paint with crisscross strokes for an even finish. Apply two thin coats instead of one thick coat, which could dry unevenly.

During breaks wrap wet brushes or rollers in plastic. For an overnight break, just place the wrapped tools in the refrigerator, rather than spending time cleaning them at day's end.

> removing wallpaper

Put money in your pocket by ridding walls of personal style statements.

YOU WILL NEED

- > Drop cloths
- > Spiker or paper scorer (available at home centers)
- > Plastic gloves and goggles
- > Wallpaper stripper
- > Large sponge, brush, roller, or spray bottle
- > Wallpaper scraper or metal putty knife

1 **Put down drop cloths** (or old sheets) to protect your floor from drips.

2 **Gently perforate** the existing wallpaper with the spiker or paper scorer. These tools are designed to cut the paper and allow the stripper to seep underneath to loosen the wallcovering. Be careful, because they can damage drywall underneath the wallpaper. (They're not as harmful to plaster walls.)

3 **Prepare the stripper** according to the manufacturer's directions. You can purchase it as a gel or in liquid and powder forms, which are added to a plastic bucket of hot water. Work in a well-ventilated area and wear gloves and goggles to prevent eye and skin irritations. Apply stripper to the walls with the sponge, brush, roller, or spray bottle. Saturate and work with just a few square yards of wallpaper at a time to prevent the stripper from drying out.

4 **Let the paper soak for a few minutes** (or longer, if the manufacturer recommends it), then use the scraper to pull up an edge of the paper; most of it will pull up easily after that. Clean up as you go to keep the stripped paper from drying on your drop cloths.

5 **Thoroughly wash and rinse the walls** before painting to remove adhesive residue left by the wallpaper. To determine if glue remains, wet the wall. Any slimy areas indicate that adhesive remains. Patch any holes or gouges with surfacing compound, then roll on a primer to prepare the walls for a coat of paint.

TIP: Stubborn wallpaper may require extra soaking or even steaming. In especially tough cases, call a wallpaper manufacturer or local store for advice.

> on a roll

If you're lucky, the wallpaper you're removing will be vinyl, which tends to be easier to remove. Many vinyl wallcoverings simply peel off in one large strip. Use a wallpaper scraper to lift a corner of the wallcovering, then pull firmly on the paper. If the vinyl has a paper backing, as some do, it may remain on the wall and you'll need to wet it to remove it. After you've peeled all the paper away, wash the walls to remove adhesive residue.

> floors

When it comes to getting a lot of bang for your buck, look down. An updated floor lifts the mood of the room and elevates your asking price. If your flooring screams dated—for example, it's covered with red shag carpeting or gold linoleum—you really only have one option: Replace it. Come sale time, you'll recoup much more than you spent, and the instant gratification will make you wonder why you didn't do it before.

The good news with flooring is that it doesn't have to wallop the wallet. Time and again the *Designed to Sell* team has added kitchen and bathroom floors for under $100, sometimes even under $50. The secret weapon? Peel-and-stick vinyl tiles. Widely available at home centers, these self-adhesive tiles mimic the look of sought-after stone and are available in solid colors to complement many styles. (See "Installing Vinyl Tiles," opposite.) And don't forget paint: You can transform a stained garage floor or cement slab with a coat of floor paint.

WOOD FLOORS

Hardwood floors score big with buyers. If you know wood floors are lurking under your carpet, consider ripping up the carpet—just so long as you have the time and money to deal with floors that may need refinishing. If the floor gods aren't smiling upon you, you may find discolored floors with difficult-to-remove pet stains. Refinishing a hardwood floor is a messy job—one that's best left to a professional or skilled do-it-yourselfer.

Not only should floors look good, they should sound good. In older houses in particular, wood floors can be squeaky—not exactly music to buyers' ears. If

possible silence the squeak from below by watching the boards from the basement while someone walks on the noisy spot. If the subfloor moves, insert a tapered shim to tighten the loose board. Dip the tip of the shim in glue, and tap it between the joist and subfloor until it's snug. If there is no movement, the finish floor probably is loose and needs to be pulled down with screws. From below drill pilot holes through the subfloor and into the finish floor at the noisy spot. Insert 1¼-inch roundhead screws.

Squeaks also can be squelched from above the floor. Drill pilot holes at 45-degree angles through the finished wood floor into the subfloor. Drive in ring-shank, spiral, or cement-coated flooring nails, which should not pull loose like smooth nails would. Use a nail set to countersink the nailheads about ⅛ inch below the surface of the floor. Fill the holes with wood putty.

CARPETING

Wall-to-wall carpeting may not have the appeal of a beautiful wood floor, but it's the norm in many homes. At a minimum carpet needs to be clean. A professional cleaning will lift dirt and fluff matted

areas, making the carpet appear newer. Often, cleaning isn't enough. Odors can linger and cleaning won't, of course, transform a forest green turf into a nice neutral surface with mass appeal.

When replacing carpeting, choose a low-cost or midrange one that has a nice look and feel. Forgo fancy plushes for more versatile uncut loop piles, such as berber, and cut-pile friezes, where the individual tufts of yarn are clearly visible. Carpets that combine cut- and loop-pile yarns to create sculptured effects also are popular, and have the bonus of camouflaging stains better. If your budget doesn't allow for replacing all the carpet, have it installed in key rooms, such as the master bedroom and family room.

> installing vinyl tiles

Let self-adhesive tiles stick it to floors stuck in a time warp.

YOU WILL NEED

> Tape measure
> Chalk line and chalk
> 12x12-inch self-adhesive vinyl tile squares
> Cardboard, paper, or tracing paper
> Utility knife
> Straightedge
> Vinyl tile cutter (optional)
> Roller, such as one used for wallpapering, or a kitchen rolling pin

1 Remove furniture, any appliances, and any molding strips along baseboards. Sweep and wash the floor; it must be level and free of wax, grease, oil, dust, and grime. Most self-adhesive tiles can be installed over well-bonded resilient floors, dry concrete, and wood floors; check manufacturer's guidelines for your specific tiles. Test the bond by placing a tile in a closet or out-of-way area.

2 Snap chalk lines to indicate the center of the floor. To do this, measure and mark the center point between the two longest parallel walls, then mark guidelines for the centers of opposite walls. Place rows of tile in both directions from the center to get an idea of positioning and how things will balance at the borders.

3 Begin the installation by peeling the paper backing from a tile. Starting where the perpendicular chalk lines cross, press the tile into place, aligning the edges with the chalk lines. Getting the first tile in the proper position is key, so be sure it's correct before proceeding. Press firmly. Starting in the center of the room and working in smaller quadrants, install tiles in a stair-step fashion, positioning them so the arrows on the back all point in the same direction. Continue to place the tiles, making sure all the edges are tightly butted.

4 To go around corners, pipes, or other areas, create a template from the cardboard, paper, or tracing paper. Trace the template onto the tile back; use the utility knife to cut the shape. To fit tiles against a wall or edge of a cabinet, lay the tile to be cut on top of the last full tile. Place another full tile against the wall or cabinet edge and mark a cutting line where the tiles overlap. Cut the tile on that line, using the utility knife and a straightedge. If desired, rent a vinyl tile cutter to help make straight cuts. For cut tiles, test the fit before removing the paper backing. When satisfied, remove the backing and press the tile into place.

5 Use a damp cloth to wipe away any adhesive that appears on the tile surface. When all the tiles are laid, use

the roller to make sure tiles are well-bonded. Reinstall molding strips and furniture. Do not wash the floor for at least five days to allow the adhesive to cure.

TIP: The paper backing on the tiles is slippery, so keep a wastebasket by your side to dispose of it as you work.

windows

Unless a room has a fireplace, the windows are usually the focal point. How you dress these features of interest has mood-altering impact. With the right window treatment, you can showcase a beautiful view to the outdoors—or block a bad one. You can make a window seem taller or wider. You can help usher in light or you can create a barrier for blindingly bright sun. From a selling standpoint, think simplicity with window coverings. Vinyl miniblinds? Definitely out!

THE READY-MADE ROUTE

Window treatments can be expensive, especially if you have lots of windows to dress. You'll need to shop smart. Look for inexpensive ready-made curtains at discount stores or on clearance tables. Get creative! The *Designed to Sell* team, for example, has fashioned stylish valances from fabric place mats. Tablecloths, bed sheets, and scarves are other options for getting yardage without a big price tag.

Many low-price window treatments are available in one length or in limited choices, but don't rule them out. If a panel is too long, hem it; if it's too short, add a border in a coordinating fabric.

Inexpensive window treatments usually don't have lining and interlining that adds body and creates a uniform appearance from the outside of the home. Therefore, make sure any window treatments you hang don't create a mishmash look from the street, which is a buyer's first impression of the state of your home.

STYLE OPTIONS

Simplicity is the goal in both the overall look, and also the specific style. You often can improve the look of a room by simply removing the "excess"—the heavy

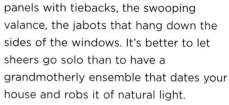

panels with tiebacks, the swooping valance, the jabots that hang down the sides of the windows. It's better to let sheers go solo than to have a grandmotherly ensemble that dates your house and robs it of natural light.

Valances—those little pieces of fabric that grace the top of a window—add softness, color, and pattern to hard architectural elements. They're usually purely decorative, and are great for sellers needing an affordable update.

Rod-pocket panels—which simply slip onto a rod—are another popular option because of their simplicity. Often these panels are made of lightweight fabric. They're widely available, and offer flexibility in how they're hung. Rather than slipping them on a rod, you can attach curtain clips with rings and slide the rings on the rod. This gives a modern look with minimal effort. Tie-up shades and Roman shades are other stylish options for staging purposes.

THE HARDWARE

Interior designer Lisa LaPorta refers to the small accessories—cabinet pulls, door knobs, light fixtures—as a home's "jewelry." Drapery hardware falls in the same category. Rods, finials, clips, and rings can give even the cheapest panel a more custom look. Choose hardware that complements the other elements in the room—say a pewter rod with a pewter chandelier. Plot your installation carefully. Hang the rod close to the ceiling, for example, to make a short window seem more prominent.

> measuring windows

Getting the right fit for window treatments ensures a polished look.

EASY UPDATE

YOU WILL NEED

> Tape measure
> Pencil
> Notepad

1 **Determine the style of window covering** and how you want to hang it. Some window treatments require being mounted inside the frame, for example.

2 **For an outside-mount window treatment,** determine the width by measuring from the outside of the window frame on one side to the outside of the frame on the other side. For the length measure from the top of the top trim of the window to the bottom of the frame, under the apron. Treatments that typically require outside-mount installation (and cover the window frame) include side panels, cafe curtains, and valances.

3 **For an inside-mount window treatment,** determine the width by measuring inside the window frame from one side to the other. For the length, measure from the top of the window, inside the frame, down the center of the window to the sill. Roman shades and blinds typically hang inside the window frame. Make sure your frames are deep enough to accommodate the brackets or other installation hardware; check the manufacturer's recommended clearance.

4 **For tab- and loop-top treatments**, add an extra 4–7 inches to the length to ensure that the treatment is mounted high enough so only the wall, not the window frame or the glass, shows between the tabs or loops.

5 **For rod-pocket and pleated treatments**, measure from the top of the window frame to either the floor or the sill, depending on the desired length. Consider how deep pleats and hems will be, and add inches accordingly.

TIP: Valances should not cover more than a third of the window length for balance. Side panels should break at the floor, rather than puddle on it, for a clean look.

> showered in style

Remember the bathroom! Window treatments can be used to create stylish frames for a shower or tub. Lisa, in fact, treats shower/tub areas like they're actually windows. A curtain gracefully draped across a tub adds a luxurious touch in the lackluster baths she often confronts. (For function, team the fabric curtain with a plastic shower liner.) Lisa prefers to use fabric that is double the width of the opening for the most drama, but her budget often limits her to using 1½ times the width. Hang the fabric curtain on its own tension rod; if desired, mount it near the ceiling for even more attention-getting style.

resources

Episode 307, pgs. 38-43, 106-111

paint
Lowe's (ph. 800-445-6937; www.lowes.com): living room bookcases, Dunn Edwards' Navaho White; living room walls, Behr's Riviera Sand, 320 E-3; kitchen walls, Valspar's Skyline Silver, 94-41B.

lighting
Home Depot U.S.A., Inc. (ph. 770-433-8211; www.homedepot.com): kitchen under-cabinet lights, 034378380056.
The Great Indoors (ph. 888-511-1155; www.thegreatindoors.com): dining room chandelier, 403408863.
Wal-Mart (ph. 800/881-9180; www.walmart.com): living room lamp set.
Target Stores (ph. 800-800-8800; www.target.com): shades for dining room chandelier, 074080535.

flooring
Lowe's (ph. 800-445-6939; www.lowes.com): vinyl tile in kitchen, Eurostone.

furniture
Coaster Company of America (ph. 800-221-9699): living room coffee table, 4895, two lounge chairs, 8108, and sofa, 8110; dining room table and chairs, 3589, 3579.

window treatments
The Linen Outlet (ph. 866-266-2728; www.strouds.com): kitchen valances, Victoria-Oyster; living room valances, 822167.
Target Stores (ph. 800-800-8800; www.target.com): living room curtain rods, 068050621, and window scarves, 068030691.

accessories
IKEA (ph. 800-434-4532 in the U.S.; 800-661-9807 in Canada; www.ikea.com): palm tree in living room, Ravenea, 70038127.

Episode 308, pgs. 44-49, 164-168

paint
Home Depot U.S.A., Inc. (ph. 770-433-8211; www.homedepot.com): living room walls, Ralph Lauren's Tangier Island; front gate, Home Depot paint color-matched to Dunn Edwards' Crayon Abyss, DE 3166; mailbox spray paint, Rustoleum's Brushed Nickel.

lighting
Lamps Plus (ph. 800-782-1967; www.lampsplus.com): uplights for living room plants, 63413; exterior lantern, Stanford Collection, 53061.

furniture
Homerica (ph. 562-903-5668; www.homelegance.com): living room TV cabinet: Rustic Pine RV Armoire, 1354-7.

window treatments
The Linen Outlet (ph. 866-266-2728; www.strouds.com): living room sheers, 828804.

accessories and miscellaneous
Home Depot U.S.A., Inc. (ph. 770-433-8211; www.homedepot.com): front doors for house, 36x80 slab door with window lites; lattice for gate, 768747106019; gate posts, 095043211087.
Lowe's (ph. 800-445-6937; www.lowes.com): gate entry set, Kwikset's Camelot-Georgian, 173853; 4-inch satin brass address numbers, 212632.
IKEA (ph. 800-434-4532 in the U.S.; ph. 800-661-9807 in Canada; www.ikea.com): living room plants/trees, 90038126.
Cost Plus World Market (ph. 310-441-5115; www.costplus.com): living room pots and planters, 000344486.

Episode 309, pgs. 32-37, 118-123, 138-143

paint
Lowe's (ph. 800-445-6937; www.lowes.com): living room walls, Valspar Oatlands Gold Bluff 94-5B; bathroom walls, Valspar Lyndhurst Gallery Beige 94-8A; bedroom walls, Valspar Lyndhurst Stone 94-3A; bedroom beams, Valspar Lyndhurst Rich Brown 93-13A.

lighting
T.J. Maxx (ph. 800-285-6299; www.tjmaxx.com): wall-mount candleholder in bathroom, 326367.
Lowe's (ph. 800-445-6937; www.lowes.com): living room and bedroom sconces, 139617.

flooring
Lowe's (ph. 800-445-6937; www.lowes.com): vinyl tile for bathroom floor, Eurostone, 185390.

furniture
The May Department Stores Company (ph. 888-666-0767; www.robinsonsmay.com): living room love seats, 12423992.
Coaster Company of America (ph. 800-221-9699): living room coffee table, 5752, and sofa table, 5753.

window treatments, fabrics, and bedding
Home Fabrics (ph. 213-689-9600): fabric for living room cornice boxes, draperies, and pillows; velvet day bed cover for bedroom.
The Great Indoors (ph. 888-511-1155; www.thegreatindoors.com): bedding ensemble, 97799900, with coordinating draperies, 97793900, and throw pillows, 97808900 and 97806900.
Lowe's (ph. 800-445-6937; www.lowes.com): living room and bedroom drapery rods, 215650.
Anna's Linens (ph. 866-266-2728; www.annaslinens.com): bedroom sheers, 2331.

accessories and miscellaneous
Big Lots (www.biglots.com): living room framed mirrors, 2133450083057.
IKEA (ph. 800-434-4532 in the U.S.; 800-661-9807 in Canada; www.ikea.com): living room tree, 70038127.
Target Stores (ph. 800-800-8800; www.target.com): three living room candleholders, 065091531, 065091526.
Home Depot U.S.A., Inc. (ph. 770-433-8211; www.homedepot.com): shower door, 087206811050.
Lowe's (ph. 800-445-6937; www.lowes.com): bathroom towel bar, Preston, 169472, and toilet-paper holder, Preston, 169465.
Anna's Linens (ph. 866-266-2728; www.annaslinens.com): bath towels, 807743, and washcloths, 807745.

Episode 310, pgs. 50-55, 112-117

paint
Lowe's (ph. 800-445-6937; www.lowes.com): kitchen walls, Valspar, Cliveden Sandstone 94-3B.

lighting
Lowe's (ph. 800-445-6937; www.lowes.com): kitchen ceiling light fixtures, 170582.

window treatments
The Great Indoors (ph. 888-511-1155; www.thegreatindoors.com): living room draperies with matching bolster, Hamlet by Sheridan.

accessories and miscellaneous
Marshalls (ph. 888-627-7425; www.marshallsonline.com): chenille throw in living room, 01654962; living room planter, 016640276; living room statue, 016523573; red plate in living room, 005989452; green vase, 003710795; lemon bottle, 016663091; yellow plate, 015188814; framed art pieces in kitchen, 005878727; rooster plate, 00507856; wall-mounted candleholders, 015802172.
Lowe's (ph. 800-445-6937; www.lowes.com): kitchen door handle and deadbolt, 173960 and 3884; kitchen flowers, 51813; red plant in living room, 96201.
Home Depot U.S.A., Inc. (ph. 770-433-8211; www.homedepot.com): French door in kitchen, 723647371516; sealant for living room fireplace, Jasco Tile Gloss and Seal, 567737.
Ross Dress for Less: living room clock, 406406403597; yellow ceramic acorn in kitchen, 406405536258.
Transworld Tile Inc.: kitchen countertop, Daltile 8100 and D100.
IKEA (ph. 800-434-4532 in the U.S.; 800-661-9807 in Canada; www.ikea.com): living room tree, Ravenea; kitchen baskets, Bastant; yellow pot in kitchen, Plommon.

Episode 311, pgs. 56-61, 170-175

paint
Lowe's (ph. 800-445-6937; www.lowes.com): garage floor paint, Rustoleum's Epoxy Shield Garage Floor Coating, 16697; living room/dining room front door and fireplace paint, Valspar's Lyndhurst Rich Brown 93-13A.

furniture
Coaster Company of America (ph. 800-221-9699): dining table, 6001, and chairs, 3656; living room coffee table, 3788.
Lowe's (ph. 800-445-6937; www.lowes.com): garage shelves, Durashelf, 43008.

window treatments
EXPO Design Center (ph. 626-256-6160; www.expo.com): dining room and living room draperies, Interior Concepts Kendra, three-in-one rod-pocket panel, 755675004850.
Target Stores (ph. 800-800-8800; www.target.com): dining room and living room drapery rods, 068070422 and 068070421.

accessories and miscellaneous
Big Lots (www.biglots.com): dining room candelabra, Iron Chandelier Taper Holder, 1453400131785.
HomeGoods (ph. 800-614-4663; The TJX Companies): dining room art, 042356; two living room lamps, 187381.
Lowe's (ph. 800-445-6937; www.lowes.com): lock set for front door, Tahoe-style lock, 181562; 14-gallon Rubbermaid Roughneck storage totes in garage, 002020374.

Episode 312, pgs. 62-67, 100-105, 156-161

paint
ICI Paints (ph. 440-826-5455; www.icipaintstores.com): bedroom walls, Dulux Prairie House 642/30YY60-205.
Home Depot U.S.A., Inc. (ph. 770-433-8211; www.homedepot.com): living room and dining room walls, Ralph Lauren's Tangier Island NA05.
Dunn Edwards Paint Stores (ph. 888-337-2468; www.dunnedwards.com): kitchen paint, Tan Moccasin 3179.

lighting
Lowe's (ph. 800-445-6937; www.lowes.com): kitchen light fixtures, Portfolio Nickel, 161851.
Coaster Company of America (ph. 800-221-9699): bedroom table lamps, 1799.

furniture
Coaster Company of America (ph. 800-221-9699): living room sofa and two chairs, 8899 and 8897; kitchen bar table and chairs, 4927 and 4926.
IKEA (ph. 800-434-4532 in the U.S.; 800-661-9807 in Canada; www.ikea.com): cube for living room coffee table, Hol 97322800; living room wall shelves, Lack 83918107.

window treatments and bedding
Anna's Linens (ph. 866-266-2728;

www.annaslinens.com): living room drapery panels, Sedona in Nubuck, 816328; place mats for kitchen window treatments, Nevada Canyon 11190; bedroom bedding ensemble, Embarcadero Belvedere collection 831528, with coordinating draperies, 8315535, and valances, 831534.
The Great Indoors (ph. 888-511-1155 www.thegreatindoors.com): dining room drapery panels in Brick with grommets, 14429, SKU 495.
Anawalt Lumber (ph. 818-769-4421)
Home Fabrics (ph. 213-689-9600): building supplies and fabric for custom-built cornice boxes in living room, no style or item numbers available for tracking specific fabric or supplies.

accessories and miscellaneous
Pride Enterprises, Inc. (ph. 818-764-4100): kitchen countertop in Almond.
IKEA (ph. 800-434-4532 in the U.S.; 800-661-9807 in Canada; www.ikea.com): candleholders, Kild Vase 9, 30087426; vase, Falang Vase 11, 00072153; poster, Natural Blues, 30078974; frame, Clips, 50070566; glass pot, Sandel 00075750; sticks in living room, Smycka 10071558; kitchen cabinet handles, Bisats 20061498; poster art, 30078993; art frame, Ram 70042676; red vase, Klave 80027741; art, 10079385; frame in dining room, Clips, 10028843.
Target Stores (ph. 800-800-8800; www.target.com): red and green chargers for living room shelves and dining room wall, 067021479 and 200011051.
Anna's Linens (ph. 866-266-2728; www.annaslinens.com): place mats for kitchen table, Nevada Canyon 11190; napkins, Nevada Canyon 809881.
Costco (www.costco.com): yellow faux suede pillow in living room, 784068.

Episode 402, pgs. 68-73, 130-135, 144-149
paint
Home Depot U.S.A., Inc. (ph. 770-433-8211; www.homedepot.com): living room and most bedroom walls, Ralph Lauren's Tangier Island NA05; bedroom accent wall, Pratt & Lambert's Almond Toast; bathroom walls, Behr's French Castle 770-A3.
lighting
The Great Indoors (ph. 888-511-1155; www.thegreatindoors.com): living room chandelier, Triarch International, 33054; bedroom chandelier, AFL Lighting, 3900-6H; bedroom lamp set, 94177.
Lowe's (ph. 800-445-6937; www.lowes.com): bedroom dresser lamp, Portfolio in Bronze; bathroom vanity lights with Etruscan glass shades, Portfolio.
furniture
Coaster Company of America (ph. 800-221-9699): dining table,

7901; dining chairs, 4466; side chairs, 3615; living room coffee table, 7619.
window treatments
Anna's Linens (ph. 866-266-2728; www.annaslinens.com): living room drapery panels in Gold, 813593; dining chair slipcloths, Gold, 832171; pillows, 829942, 829944, 829935 and 829947; chair slipcover, 832364.
Home Fabrics (ph. 213-689-9600): fabric for drapery panels; animal print grid fabric for ottoman; animal print desk chair and pillow fabric.
Target Stores (ph. 800-800-8800; www.target.com): living room curtain rods, Ramona, antique bronze, 233434-125.
Big Lots (www.biglots.com): bedroom curtain rods, 42437012133.
The Linen Outlet: (ph. 866-266-2728; www.strouds.com): duvet used as fabric for cornice boxes in bedroom, Baronial Manor, 740845037747.
accessories
The Great Indoors (ph. 888-511-1155; www.thegreatindoors.com): bathroom vase, 11199; bathroom cabinet knobs, 20419.
Marshalls: (ph. 888-627-7425; www.marshallsonline.com): iron art piece above living room mantel, 017198051; iron sconces in bedroom, 017186186.
Lowe's (ph. 800-445-6937; www.lowes.com): bathroom toilet paper holder, Stamford.
IKEA (ph. 800-434-4532 in the U.S.; 800-661-9807 in Canada; www.ikea.com): art, Tvilling, 70078096; living room frames, Fanaholm, 50055735; bathroom shower curtain, Felicia, 70078062.
Big Lots (www.biglots.com): bathroom shower curtain tension rod, 1463500191274.
The Linen Outlet: (ph. 866-266-2728; www.strouds.com): bedroom duvet and shams, Baronial Manor, 740845037747 and 740845037785; bathroom washcloths, 81771; hand towels, 817719; bath towels, 817709.
Anna's Linens (ph. 866-266-2728; www.annaslinens.com): dining chair slipcovers in Gold, 832171; chair slipcovers in bedroom, 832364; bedroom pillows, 829942, 829944, 829935, and 829947.

Episode 406, pgs. 80-85, 124-129
paint
Spectra Paint Centers Inc. (ph. 888-411-7246; www.spectrapaint.com): Pratt and Lambert's Safari paint; living room paneling paint, Pratt and Lambert's Tarragon; bathroom walls, Pratt and Lambert's Muffin Tan, 2277-B1.
furniture
Coaster Company of America (ph. 800-221-9699): living room coffee table, 5421.
Michael's Furniture Warehouse (ph. 818-904-9414; www.ashleyfurniture.com): living room sofa, Cinnabar Loveseat, 5791635C.

Kmart (ph. 866-562-7848; www.bluelight.com): dining table, Lafayette, 072000827642.
IKEA (ph. 800-434-4532 in the U.S.; 800-661-9807 in Canada; www.ikea.com): wicker chairs in living room, Agen, 50058376.
lighting
Lowe's (ph. 800-445-6937; www.lowes.com): dining room chandelier, 76901; light fixtures, Leaves, 155401.
window treatments
Kmart (ph. 866-562-7848; www.bluelight.com): valances, Martha Stewart, Persian Paisley, 07665763995; pillows, 73879083206.
IKEA (ph. 800-434-4532 in the U.S.; 800-661-9807 in Canada; www.ikea.com): valances, Blenda, 10071775.
Target Stores (ph. 800-800-8800; www.target.com): valances, Fieldcrest Classic, 068032098.
accessories and miscellaneous
Big Lots (www.biglots.com): living room art, 2133450098006.
Kmart (ph. 866-562-7848; www.bluelight.com): pillows, 73879083206; bathroom shower curtain, Martha Stewart, Wide Stripe, 63676502774.
Lowe's (ph. 800-445-6937; www.lowes.com): living room mantel, Heritage, 163237; bathroom towel ring, Signature Bathware, Astina, 124065; knobs, 90764; countertop, Labrador Granite, 201969, 201995, 65433, 65579; tile, Armstrong Meadowstone, Midwestern Fantasy, 219769.
Home Depot U.S.A., Inc. (ph. 770-433-8211; www.homedepot.com): bath fixtures, Price Pfister, 8B5-8PBC; bathroom countertop, 048118392600; vinyl tile, Saratoga Slate, 317150.
Marshalls (ph. 88-627-7425; www.marshallsonline.com): bathroom mirror, 002911661.
The Linen Outlet (ph. 866-266-2728; www.strouds.com): towel, 819078.

Episode 407, pgs. 74-79, 92-97, 150-155
paint
Home Depot U.S.A., Inc. (ph. 770-433-8211; www.homedepot.com): Ralph Lauren's Cotswold Breeches; trim paint, Swiss Coffee; wall paint, Ralph Lauren's Fairy Wren.
lighting
IKEA (ph. 800-434-4532 in the U.S.; 800-661-9807 in Canada; www.ikea.com): Arstid lamps, 00013861; pillow stuffers, 30053134.
Lamps Plus (ph.800-782-1967; www.lampsplus.com): chandelier, 49405.
Lowe's (ph. 800-445-6937; www.lowes.com): light fixture, American Standard Traditions Retrospect, 95029.
Home Depot U.S.A., Inc. (ph. 770-433-8211; www.homedepot.com):

uplight, Hampton Bay Dimensions, 051138663827.
furniture
Al's Furniture Clearance Center (ph. 800-746-4237; www.alsdiscountfurniture.com): living room two-piece Microfiber tan sectional.
IKEA (ph. 800-434-4532 in the U.S.; 800-661-9807 in Canada; www.ikea.com): living room coffee table, Granas, 00073299.
window and window treatments
Home Depot U.S.A., Inc. (ph. 770-433-8211; www.homedepot.com): living room window, 60"x40" Vinyl Glider Window, 728262000391.
IKEA (ph. 800-434-4532 in the U.S.; 800-661-9807 in Canada; www.ikea.com): curtain rings, Adele, 73493680.
Bed Bath & Beyond (ph. 800-462-3966; www.bedbathandbeyond.com): tie-top drapery panels, Reflections by Bloomcraft, 48910; kitchen valances, drapes, shades.
Target Stores (ph. 800-800-8800; www.target.com): window treatments, 068030692.
accessories
Home Depot U.S.A., Inc. (ph. 770-433-8211; www.homedepot.com): plant, 087404500121; plant tray, 087404510120.
Bed Bath & Beyond (ph. 800-462-3966; www.bedbathandbeyond.com): barstool covers.
Marshalls (ph. 88-627-7425; www.marshallsonline.com): bedding, Quilt, 009112508; striped pillow, 006799252.
IKEA (ph. 800-434-4532 in the U.S.; 800-661-9807 in Canada; www.ikea.com): pillow stuffers, 30053134.

GET MORE TIPS FROM PROS

PAGE 17:
Discover great ways to attract buyers:
HGTV.com/homeselling

PAGE 21:
Learn how to get organized:
HGTV.com/organize

PAGE 33:
Highlight your fireplace:
HGTV.com/fireplace

PAGE 77:
Dress up your windows:
HGTV.com/wonderfulwindows

PAGE 89:
Experiment with furniture:
HGTV.com/roomplanner

PAGE 167:
Dress up your home's exterior:
HGTV.com/curbappeal

INDEX

to some, inspiration comes naturally.
for the rest of us, may we suggest a good book?

Make that three good books. In all three, you'll find simple and affordable design ideas, not to mention plenty of inspiration. For more great *Designed to Sell* ideas, watch the new team of B. Michael Johnson and Monica Pederson as they show viewers how to turn a tired house into a showpiece on a $2,000 budget!

YOU SHOULD SEE WHAT'S ON HGTV!

HGTV.com